History K
Student Guide

Part 2

K12

About K12 Inc.

K12 Inc. (NYSE: LRN) drives innovation and advances the quality of education by delivering state-of-the-art digital learning platforms and technology to students and school districts around the world. K12 is a company of educators offering its online and blended curriculum to charter schools, public school districts, private schools, and directly to families. More information can be found at K12.com.

978-1-60153-309-8

Printed by LSC Communications, Harrisonburg, VA, USA, May 2019.

Table of Contents

Student Guide
Lesson 1: Christopher Columbus

When Europeans arrived in North America, life changed and a new civilization began to grow and develop. Christopher Columbus led the way in North America. Pilgrims, Quakers, and others followed. Learn how the first 13 colonies grew along the Atlantic coast, while a Spanish priest began building missions in the West.

In 1492, Christopher Columbus sailed across the Atlantic searching for a western route from Europe to Asia. [NGT]He never found one, but [NGT]he did discover what the Europeans called the "New World," which helped to open up a new age of European exploration.

Lesson Objectives

- Identify Christopher Columbus as a person who sailed west from Europe in 1492.
- Explain that Columbus called the people he met "Indians" because he thought he had reached the islands that Europeans called "the Indies."
- Identify the Niña, Pinta, and Santa María as Columbus's three ships.

PREPARE

Approximate lesson time is 45 minutes.

Materials

For the Student

- map of the New World

Optional

- Americas Cutout activity sheet
- Columbus's Coloring Sheet
- Oh, Columbus song sheet

globe, inflatable
crayons, 16 or more
Elmer's Glue-All
map, world
scissors, round-end safety
Follow the Dream: The Story of Christopher Columbus by Peter Sis

Keywords and Pronunciation

Niña (NEEN-yah)
Pinta (PEEN-tah)

LEARN

Activity 1: Learning About Christopher Columbus *(Online)*

Activity 2: Discovering New Lands *(Online)*

Activity 3: Sailing to the New World *(Online)*

Activity 4: Map Activity *(Online)*

Activity 5. Optional: Color Columbus's Journey *(Online)*

ASSESS

Lesson Assessment: Christopher Columbus (*Online*)

You will complete an offline assessment covering the main objectives of this lesson. Your learning coach will score this assessment.

LEARN

Activity 6. Optional: Read More About Columbus *(Online)*

New World

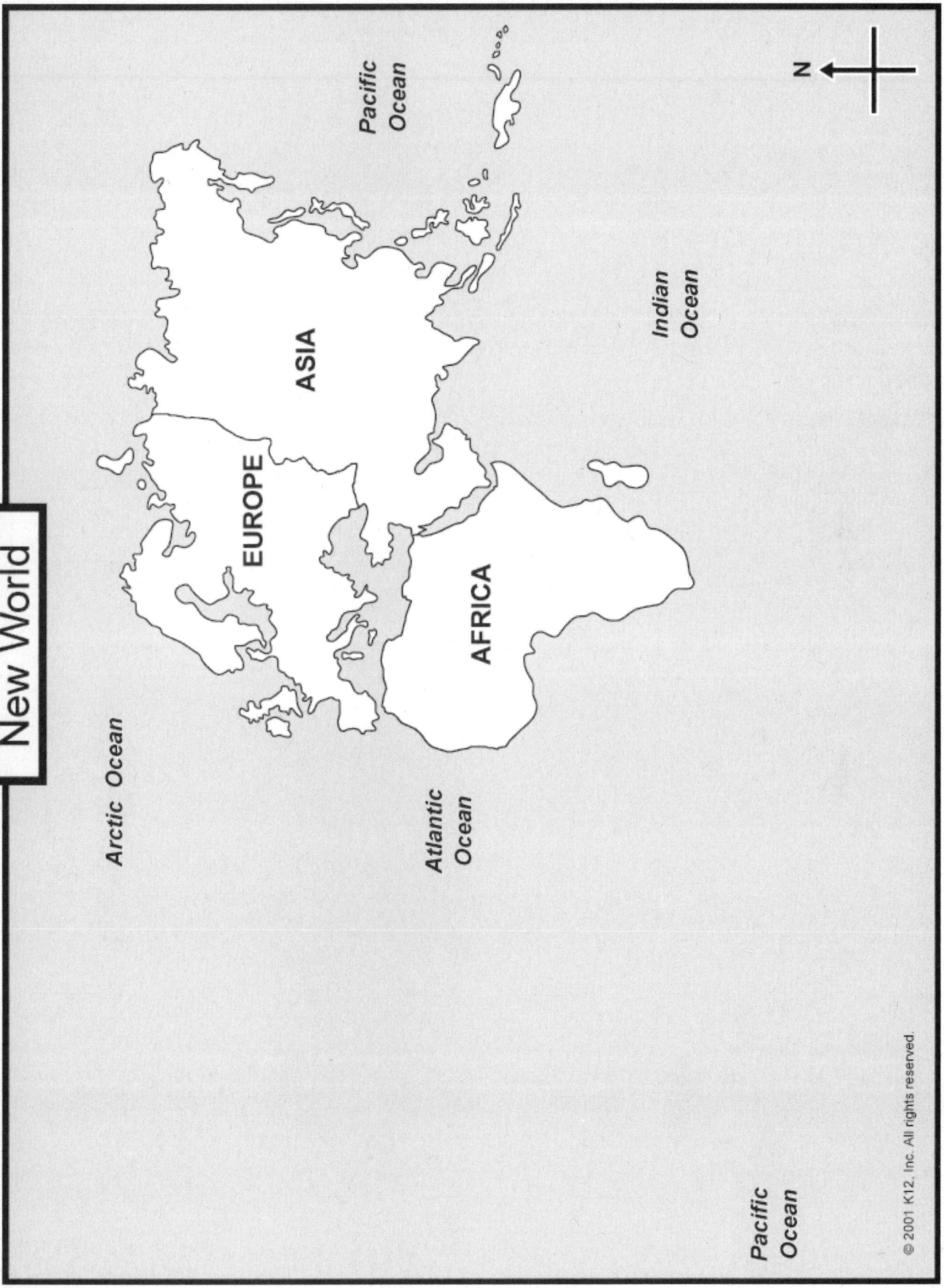
Pacific Ocean
N
ASIA
Indian Ocean
EUROPE
AFRICA
Arctic Ocean
Atlantic Ocean
Pacific Ocean
© 2001 K12, Inc. All rights reserved.

cut
NORTH AMERICA
Plymouth, Massachusetts
San Salvador
SOUTH AMERICA

Oh, Columbus

(To the tune of *Clementine*)

Oh, Columbus; oh, Columbus,
Sailed the ocean wide and blue.
Seeking Asia, found America,
In fourteen ninety-two.

In the Niña, in the Pinta,
In the Santa María, too,
Seeking Asia, found America,
In fourteen ninety-two.

Oh, Columbus; oh, Columbus,
Was so brave and wise and true,
He sailed from Spain to the Americas
In fourteen ninety-two.

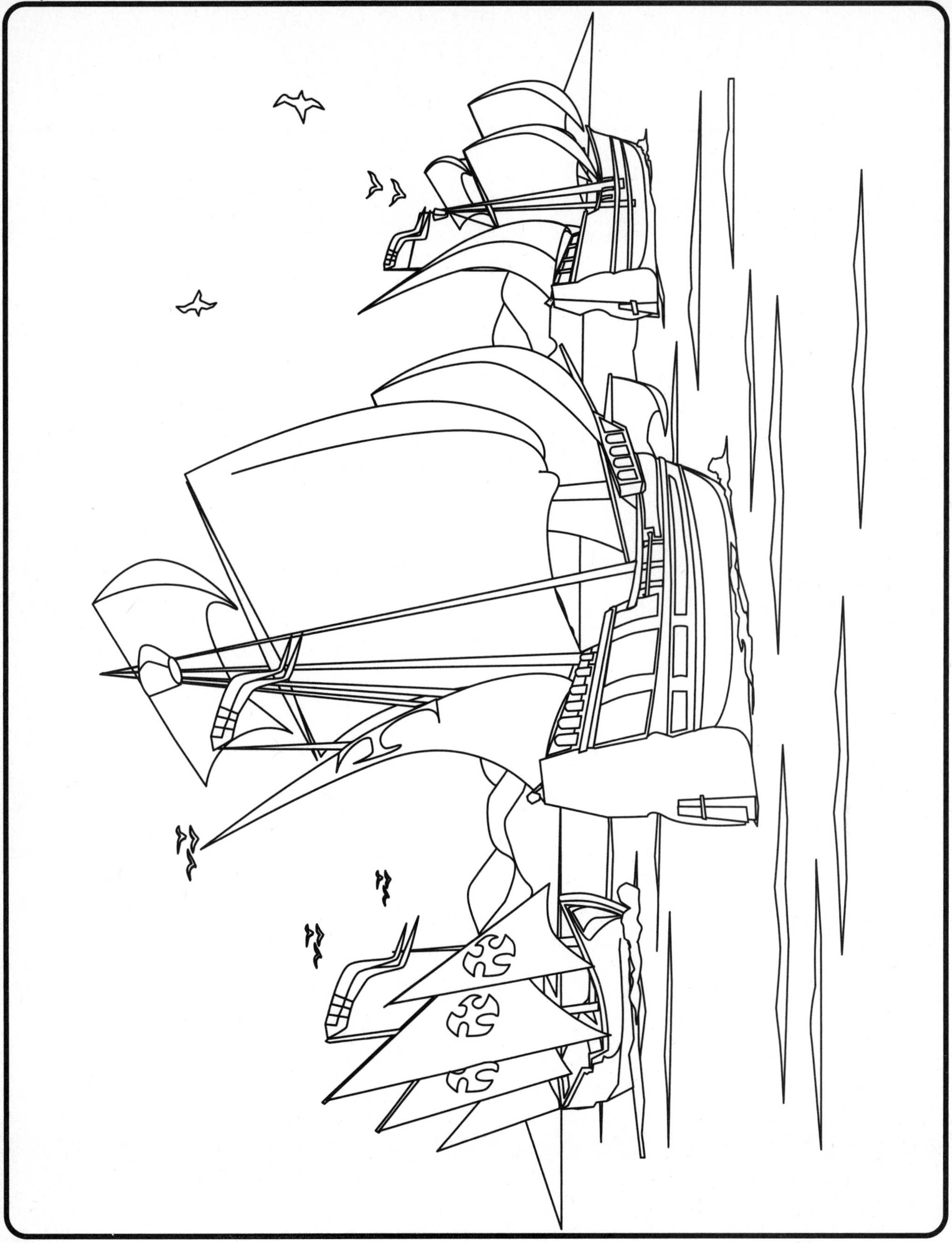

Name Date

Lesson Assessment

Christopher Columbus

1. Who sailed west from Europe in 1492?
2. Why did Columbus call the people he met "Indians"?
3. What were the names of Columbus's three ships?

Student Guide
Lesson 2: The Pilgrims' First Thanksgiving

The Pilgrims sailed to America on a ship named the *Mayflower.* They had a hard first year, but a Pawtuxet Indian named Squanto taught them skills to help them thrive in America. That autumn, the Pilgrims held a Thanksgiving feast and invited Squanto and some of the Wampanoag Indians.

Lesson Objectives

- Identify the Pilgrims as people from England who settled in America.
- Name the Mayflower as the ship on which the Pilgrims sailed to America.
- Name Squanto as the Native American who helped the Pilgrims survive.
- State that the Pilgrims and the Wampanoag Indians celebrated the first Thanksgiving together.

PREPARE

Approximate lesson time is 45 minutes.

Materials

For the Student

map of the New World

crayons, 16 or more

Optional

The First Thanksgiving activity sheet

The Pilgrims' First Thanksgiving by Ann McGovern

The Story of the Pilgrims by Katharine Ross

Keywords and Pronunciation

Samoset (SAM-uh-set)

Squanto (SKWAHN-toh)

Wampanoag (wahm-puh-NOH-ag)

LEARN

Activity 1: Columbus's Discovery *(Online)*

Activity 2: The New World *(Online)*

Activity 3: The Pilgrims' Voyage *(Online)*

Activity 4: The First Thanksgiving *(Online)*

Activity 5. Optional: Thanksgiving Celebration *(Online)*

ASSESS

Lesson Assessment: The Pilgrims' First Thanksgiving (*Online*)

You will complete an offline assessment covering the main objectives of this lesson. Your learning coach will score this assessment.

LEARN

Activity 6: Read On! *(Online)*

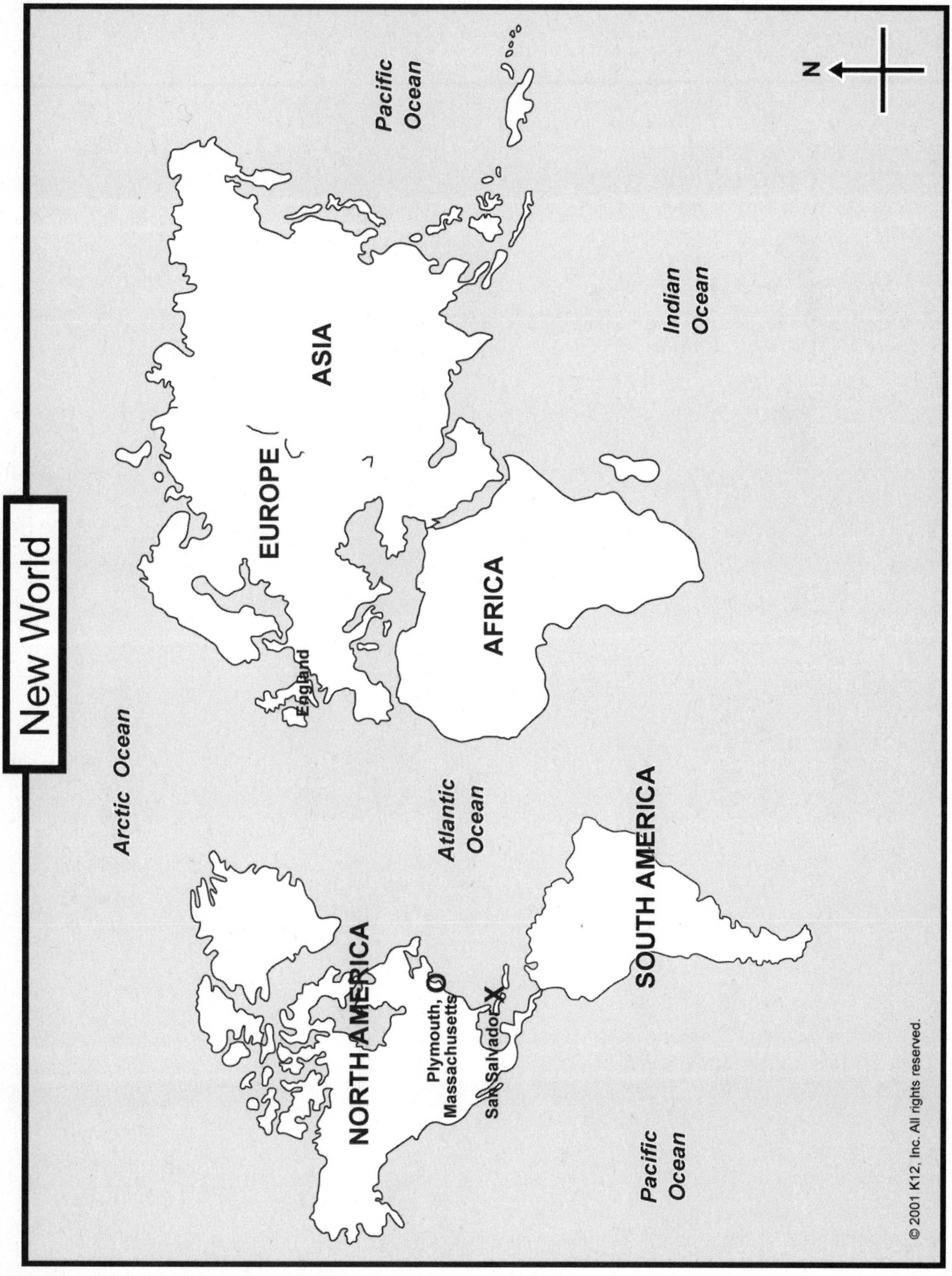
New World
N
Arctic Ocean
Pacific Ocean
Indian Ocean
Atlantic Ocean
Pacific Ocean
ASIA
EUROPE
AFRICA
England
NORTH AMERICA
SOUTH AMERICA
Plymouth, Massachusetts
San Salvador
O
X
© 2001 K12, Inc. All rights reserved.

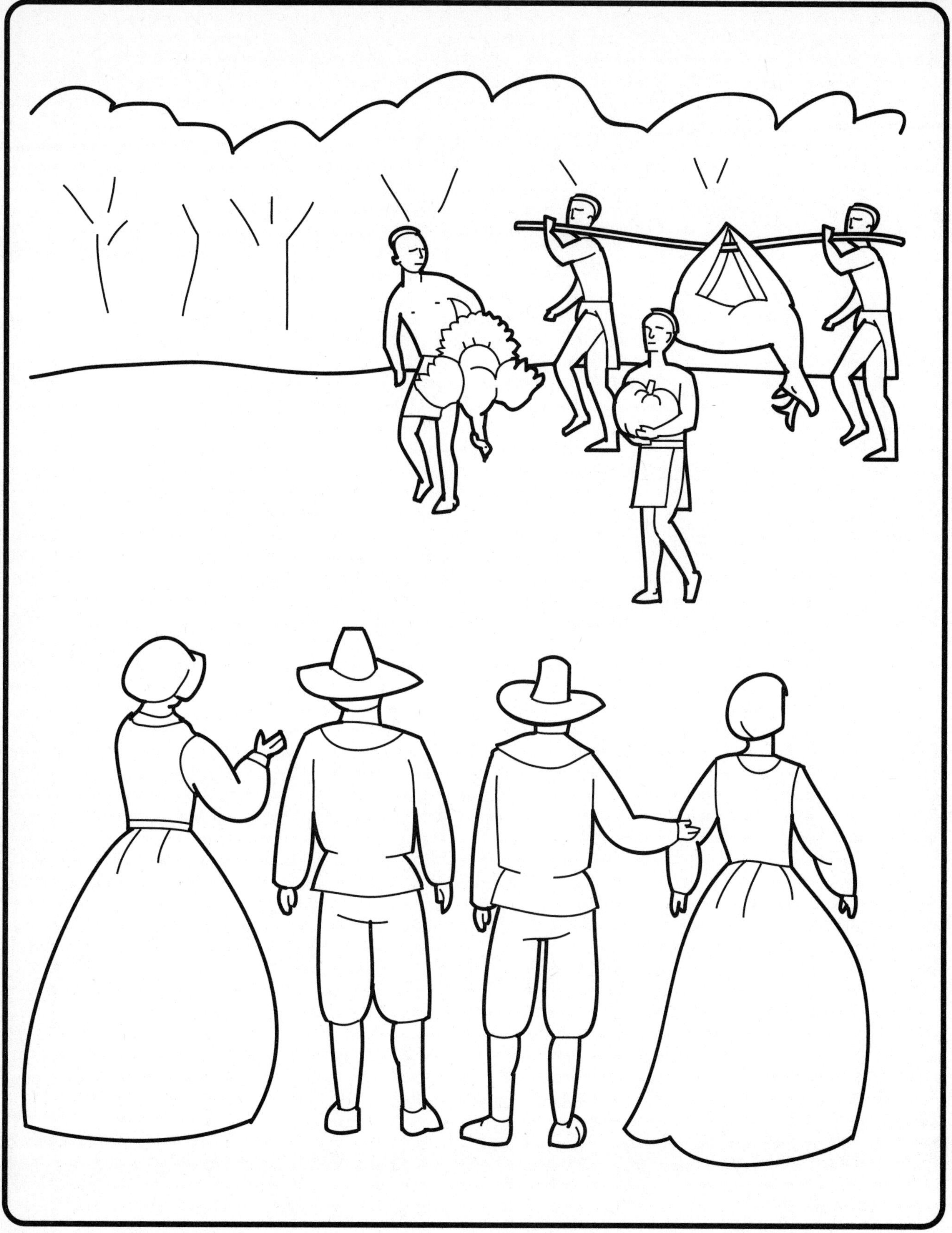

Name Date

Lesson Assessment

The Pilgrims' First Thanksgiving

1. What group of very religious people sailed from England to settle in America?
2. What was the name of the ship that brought the Pilgrims to the New World?
3. What is the name of the Native American who helped the Pilgrims survive?
4. Who celebrated the first Thanksgiving together?

Student Guide
Lesson 3: Thirteen English Colonies and the Story of William Penn

English people continued to come to America, many in search of gold and riches. William Penn chose to become a member of the Quakers, a religious group. Quakers were not treated well in England. After [NGT]his father's death, William Penn negotiated with the king to grant [NGT]him a colony in America. Together they decided to name the colony *Pennsylvania.*

Lesson Objectives

- Explain there were 13 English colonies along the Atlantic coast.
- Name William Penn as the founder of Pennsylvania.
- Know that Pennsylvania was founded for religious freedom.

PREPARE

Approximate lesson time is 45 minutes.

Materials

For the Student

- map of the New World
- map of the English Colonies
- crayons, 16 or more

Optional

- penny
- pencils, no. 2
- paper, 8 1/2" x 11"

LEARN

Activity 1: The Pilgrims *(Online)*

Activity 2: The English Colonies *(Online)*

Activity 3: William Penn's Pennsylvania *(Online)*

Activity 4: The Rest of the Thirteen Colonies *(Online)*

Activity 5. Optional: Review the Thirteen Colonies *(Online)*

ASSESS

Lesson Assessment: Thirteen English Colonies and the Story of William Penn (*Online*)

You will complete an offline assessment covering the main objectives of this lesson. Your learning coach will score this assessment.

LEARN

Activity 6. Optional: Nine Men's Morrice *(Online)*

New World

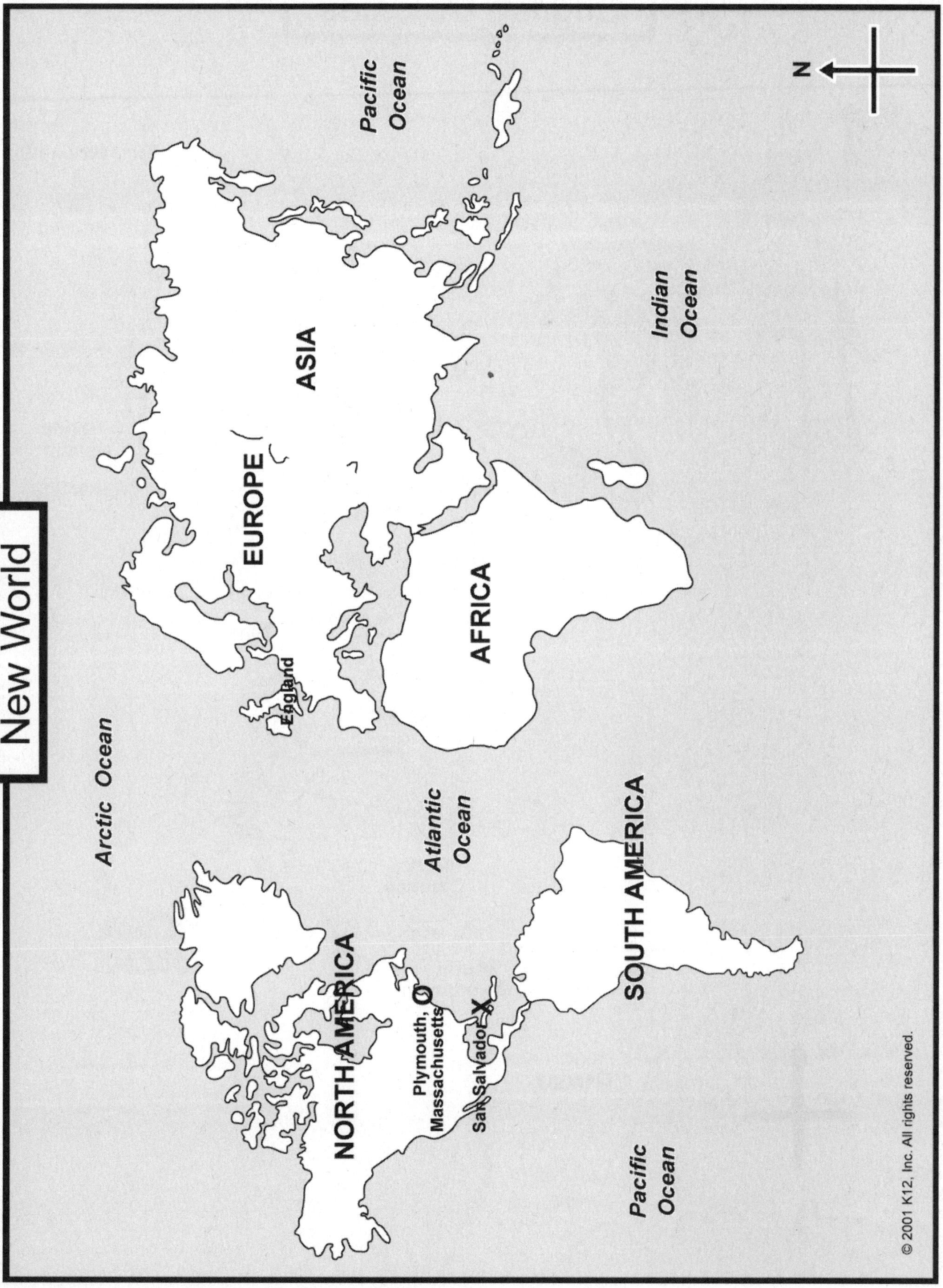
Arctic Ocean
Pacific Ocean
ASIA
EUROPE
England
AFRICA
Indian Ocean
Atlantic Ocean
NORTH AMERICA
Plymouth, Massachusetts
San Salvador
X
SOUTH AMERICA
Pacific Ocean
N
© 2001 K12, Inc. All rights reserved.

English Colonies

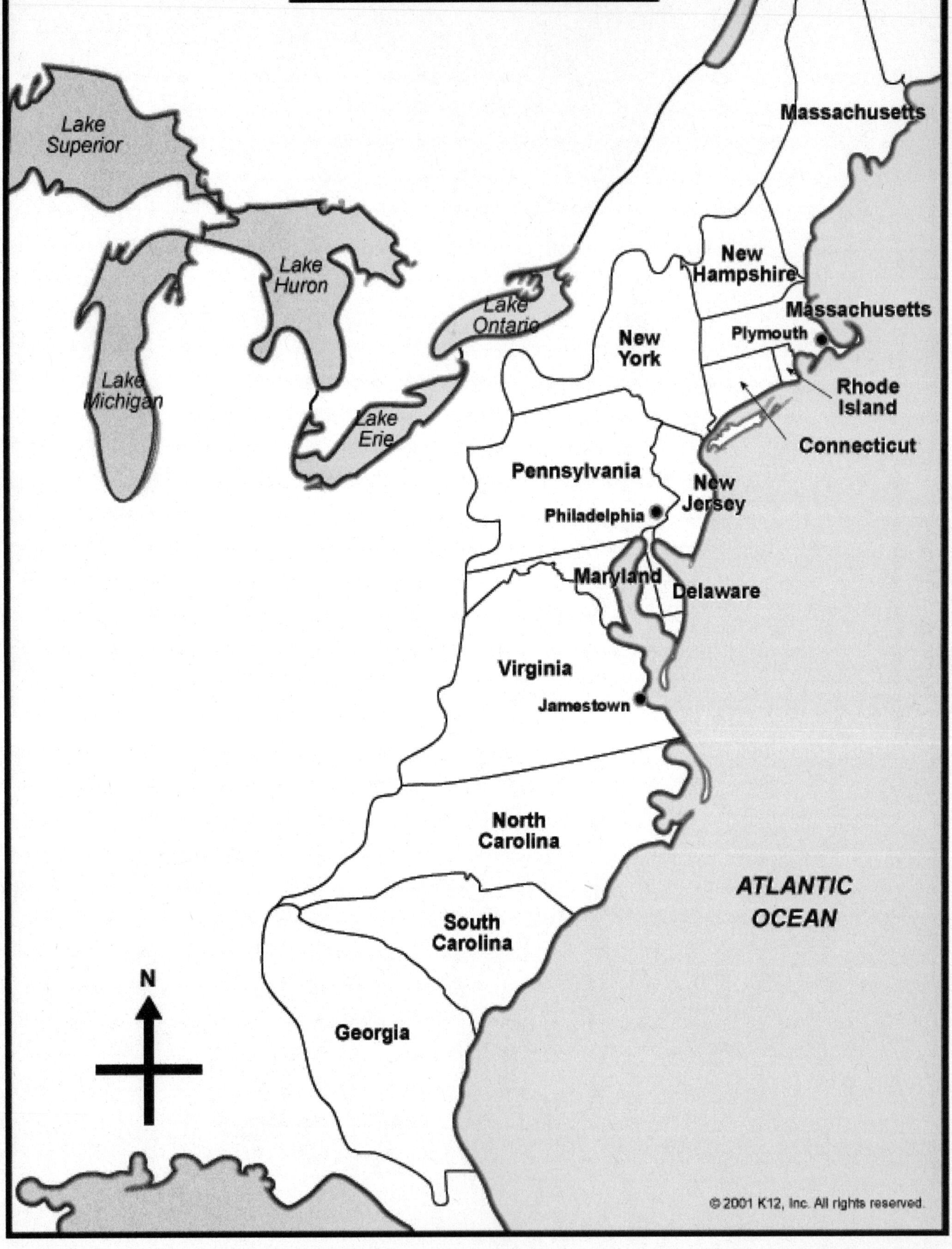
Lake Superior
Lake Michigan
Lake Huron
Lake Ontario
Lake Erie
Massachusetts
New Hampshire
Massachusetts
Plymouth
New York
Rhode Island
Connecticut
Pennsylvania
Philadelphia
New Jersey
Maryland
Delaware
Virginia
Jamestown
North Carolina
South Carolina
Georgia
ATLANTIC OCEAN
N
© 2001 K12, Inc. All rights reserved.

Name Date

Lesson Assessment

Thirteen English Colonies and the Story of William Penn

1. Who was the founder of Pennsylvania?
2. Why was Pennsylvania founded?
3. How many colonies were there?
4. What ocean did the English colonies in America lay next to?

Student Guide
Lesson 4: Junípero Serra in California

While the English colonized the Atlantic seaboard of America, the Spanish established settlements in the west. Junípero Serra, born on a small island off the coast of Spain, became a priest whose determined mission-building efforts were among the most important Spanish legacies in North America.

Lesson Objectives

- Identify Junípero Serra as a Spanish priest.
- State that Junípero Serra started missions in what is now California.

PREPARE

Approximate lesson time is 45 minutes.

Materials

For the Student

- map of English Colonies
- globe, inflatable
- map of Early Spanish Missions

Optional

- crayons, 16 or more
- Legos
- blocks

Keywords and Pronunciation

Junípero Serra (yoo-NEE-pay-roh SEHR-rah)

LEARN

Activity 1: The English Colonies *(Online)*

Activity 2: Junípero Serra's Dream *(Online)*

Activity 3: The Mission of San Diego *(Online)*

Activity 4. Optional: Junípero Serra - From Spain to California *(Online)*

ASSESS

Lesson Assessment: Junípero Serra in California (*Online*)

You will complete an offline assessment covering the main objectives of this lesson. Your learning coach will score this assessment.

LEARN

Activity 5. Optional: Building the California Missions *(Online)*

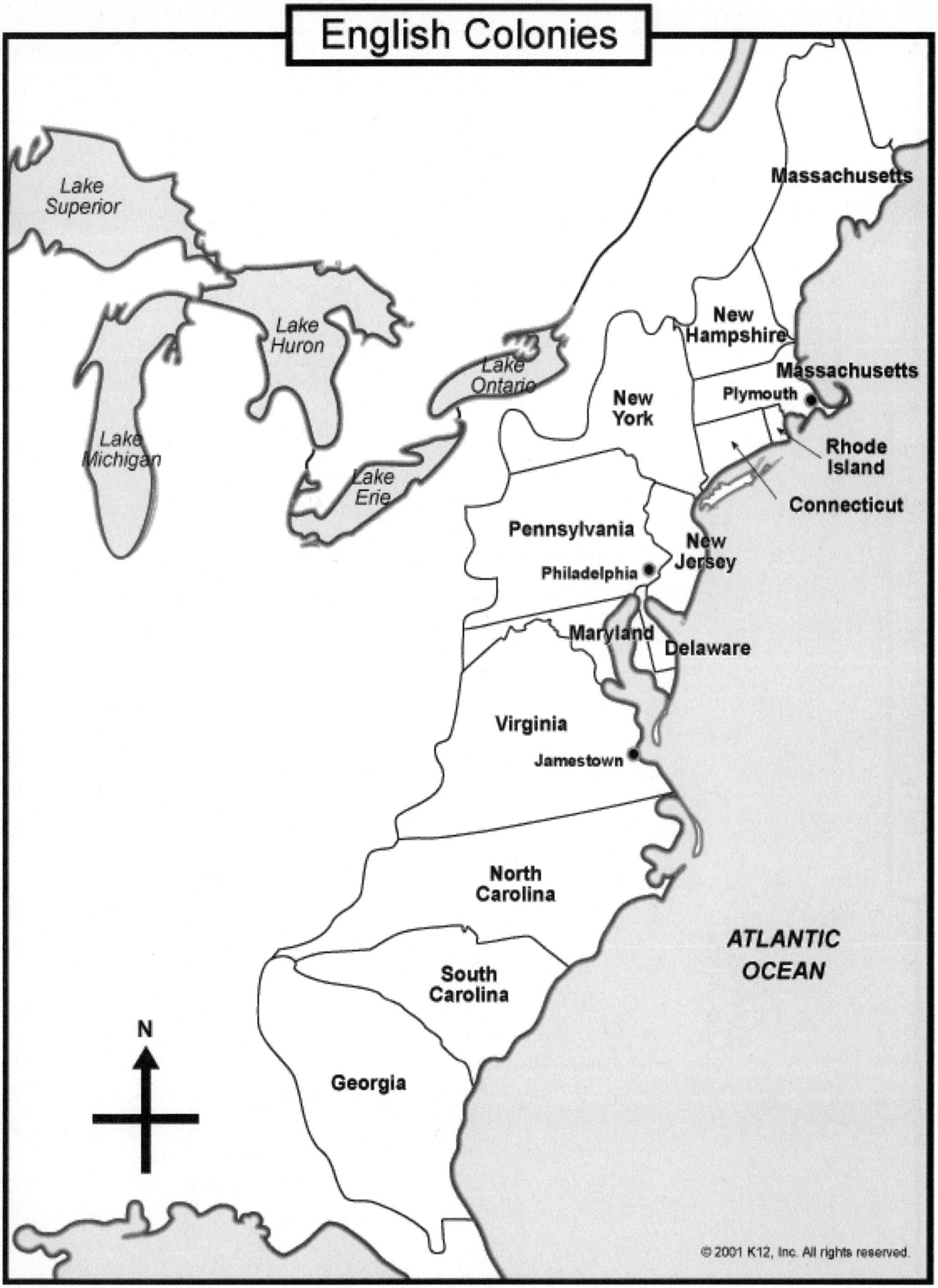
English Colonies
Lake Superior
Lake Huron
Lake Michigan
Lake Ontario
Lake Erie
Massachusetts
New Hampshire
Massachusetts
Plymouth
New York
Rhode Island
Connecticut
Pennsylvania
Philadelphia
New Jersey
Maryland
Delaware
Virginia
Jamestown
North Carolina
South Carolina
Georgia
ATLANTIC OCEAN
N
© 2001 K12, Inc. All rights reserved.

Early Spanish Missions

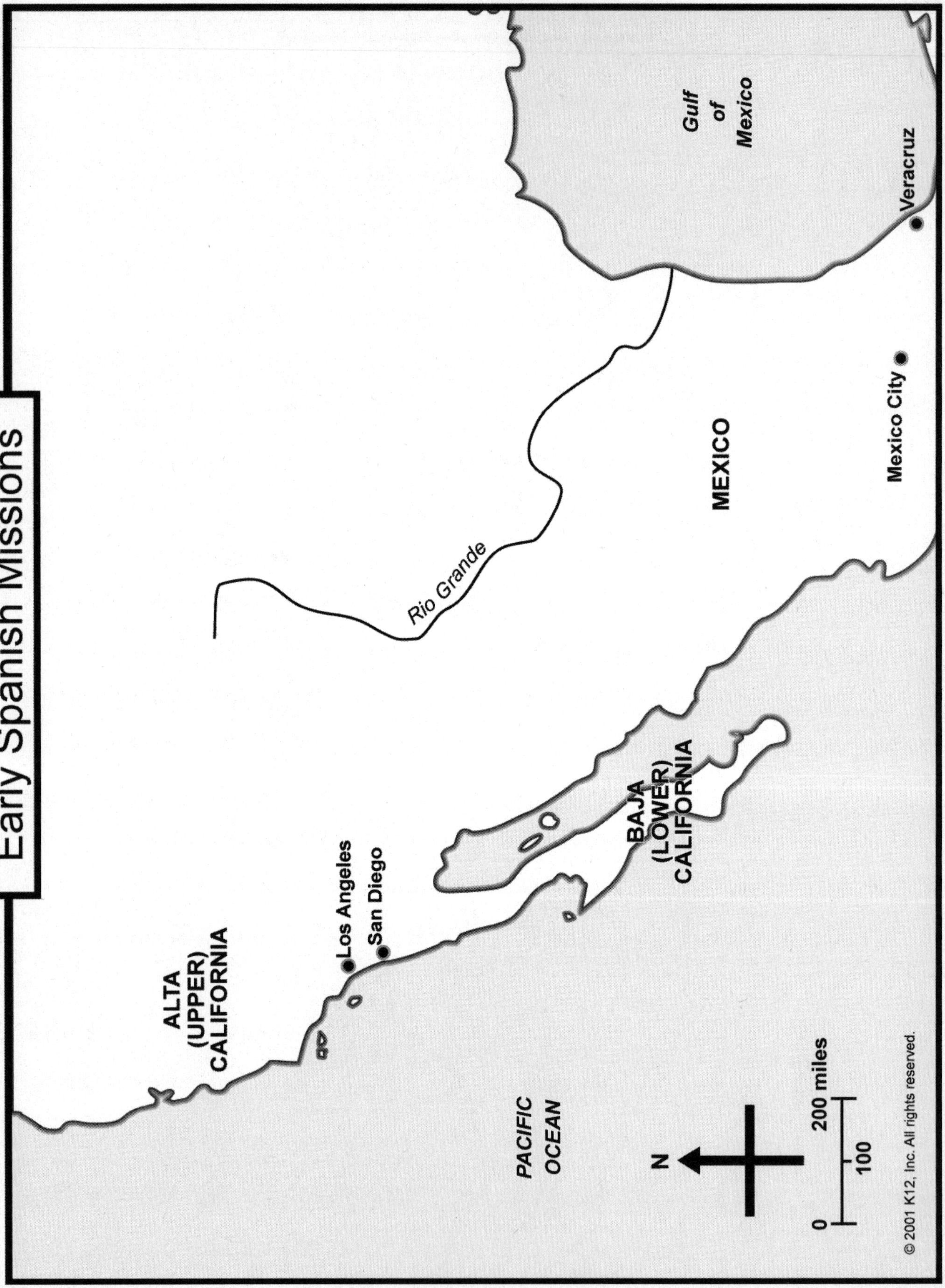

Name Date

Lesson Assessment

Junípero Serra in California

1. Who was Junípero Serra?
2. What did Junípero Serra do?

Student Guide

Lesson 1: "Yankee Doodle" - The American Revolution

Just how did America get its start as a nation? Find out as you investigate the American Revolution and the beginnings of democracy in the United States. Meet Betsy Ross, see the American flag take shape, and understand the meaning of the stars and stripes. Then learn how the leadership of George Washington and Thomas Jefferson helped shape this new nation.

After many years of colonial rule, Americans declared themselves free of England and became the United States of America, an independent country and a democracy. The war for independence is called the American Revolution.

Lesson Objectives

- State that the United States used to be 13 colonies ruled by England.
- Explain that the English colonists broke away from England and formed an independent country.
- Name the American Revolution as the war in which the United States won its independence from England.
- Identify the United States as a democracy.

PREPARE

Approximate lesson time is 45 minutes.

Materials

For the Student

map of the English Colonies

Optional

paper, colored construction, 12"x12"

scissors, round-end safety

stapler

LEARN

Activity 1: A Review of the Colonies *(Online)*

Activity 2: Let the People Rule! *(Online)*

Activity 3: Song: Yankee Doodle *(Online)*

Activity 4: Becoming a Democracy *(Online)*

Activity 5: More Yankee Doodle *(Online)*

Activity 6: A Review *(Online)*

Activity 7: Make a Patriot's Hat *(Online)*

ASSESS

Lesson Assessment: "Yankee Doodle" - The American Revolution (*Online*)

You will complete an offline assessment covering the main objectives of this lesson. Your learning coach will score this assessment.

LEARN

Activity 8. Optional: Daily Life in the Colonies *(Online)*

English Colonies
Lake Superior
Lake Huron
Lake Michigan
Lake Ontario
Lake Erie
Massachusetts
New Hampshire
Massachusetts
Plymouth
New York
Rhode Island
Connecticut
Pennsylvania
New Jersey
Philadelphia
Maryland
Delaware
Virginia
Jamestown
North Carolina
South Carolina
Georgia
ATLANTIC OCEAN
N
© 2001 K12, Inc. All rights reserved.

Name ______________________ Date ______________________

Lesson Assessment

"Yankee Doodle" - The American Revolution

1. How many colonies were there in America?

2. What country ruled the thirteen colonies?

3. When England colonists decided that they didn't want to be ruled by a king in faraway England, what did they do?

4. Instead of being ruled by a king, the United States decided to have a government where people rule themselves. What kind of government is this?

5. What is the name of the war that the American colonies fought against England to gain their independence?

Student Guide
Lesson 2: Betsy Ross and the First American Flag

The American flag flies over the nation's capital, its monuments, homes, and schools. It's even on the moon! Today we learn the well-known story of how Betsy Ross sewed the first American flag.

Lesson Objectives

- Identify the American flag as a symbol of the United States of America.
- State that the American flag has 13 red and white stripes, representing the original thirteen colonies.
- State that the American flag has 50 stars, one for each state.
- Identify Betsy Ross as the person traditionally credited with sewing the first American flag.

PREPARE

Approximate lesson time is 45 minutes.

Materials

For the Student

Optional

Five-Pointed Star activity sheet

crayons, 16 or more

paper, 8 1/2" x 11"

scissors, round-end safety

LEARN

Activity 1: Looking at the American Flag *(Online)*

Activity 2: Betsy Ross and the American Flag *(Online)*

Activity 3: Creating the American Flag *(Online)*

Activity 4: A Five-Pointed Star in a Single Snip *(Online)*

Activity 5: A Grand Old Flag *(Online)*

ASSESS

Lesson Assessment: Betsy Ross and the First American Flag (*Online*)

You will complete an offline assessment covering the main objectives of this lesson. Your learning coach will score this assessment.

LEARN

Activity 6. Optional: Learn the Pledge of Allegiance *(Online)*

Make a Five-Pointed Star

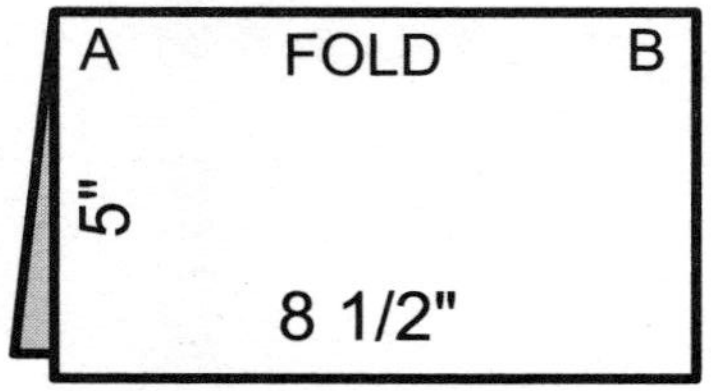

Step 1. Fold an 8 1/2" x 10" piece of paper in half.

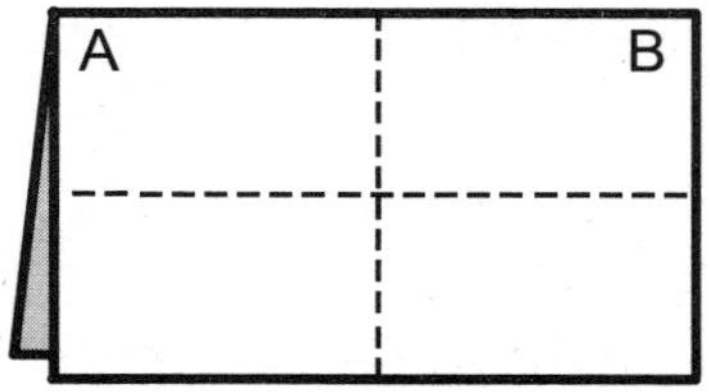

Step 2. Fold and unfold in half both ways to form creased center lines. The paper should still be folded in half.

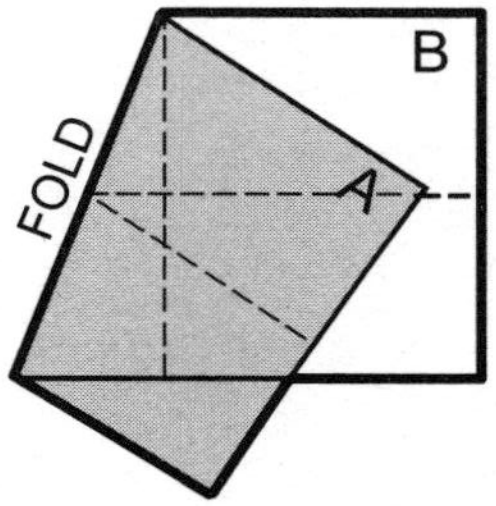

Step 3. Bring corner A right to meet the center line. Be sure to fold from the vertical crease line.

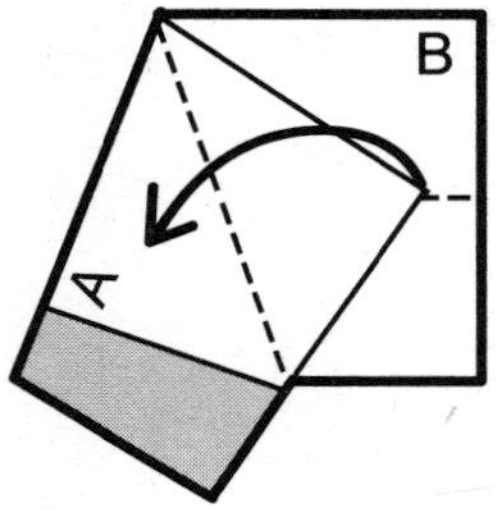

Step 4. Bring corner A left till edges come together, then make the fold.

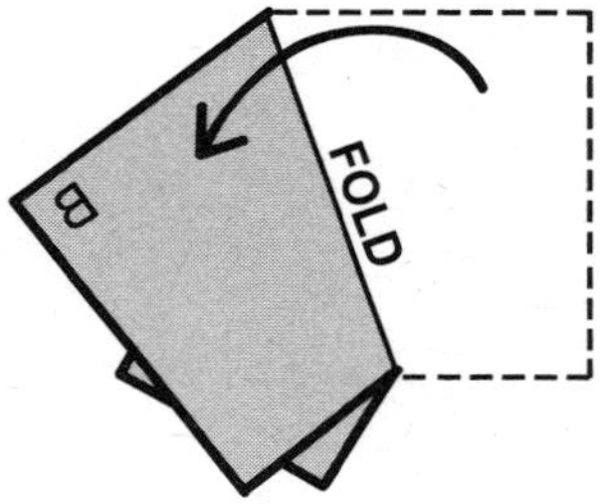

Step 5. Bring corner B left and fold.

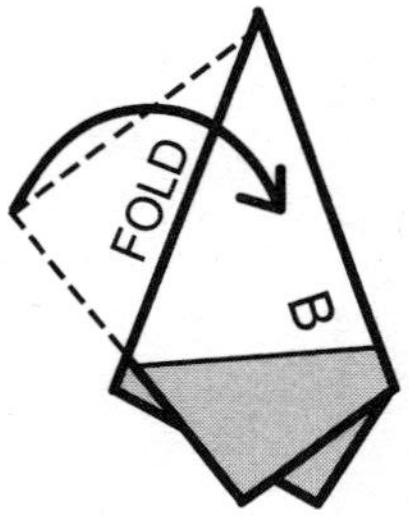

Step 6. Bring corner B right until edges come together. Then fold.

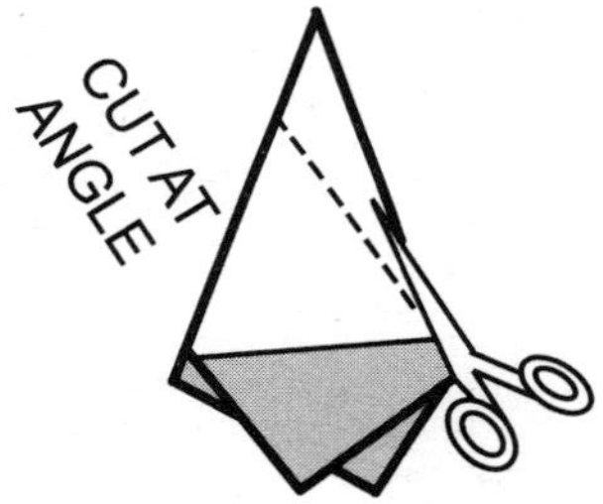

Step 7. Cut on the angle as shown in the picture. Then unfold the small piece.

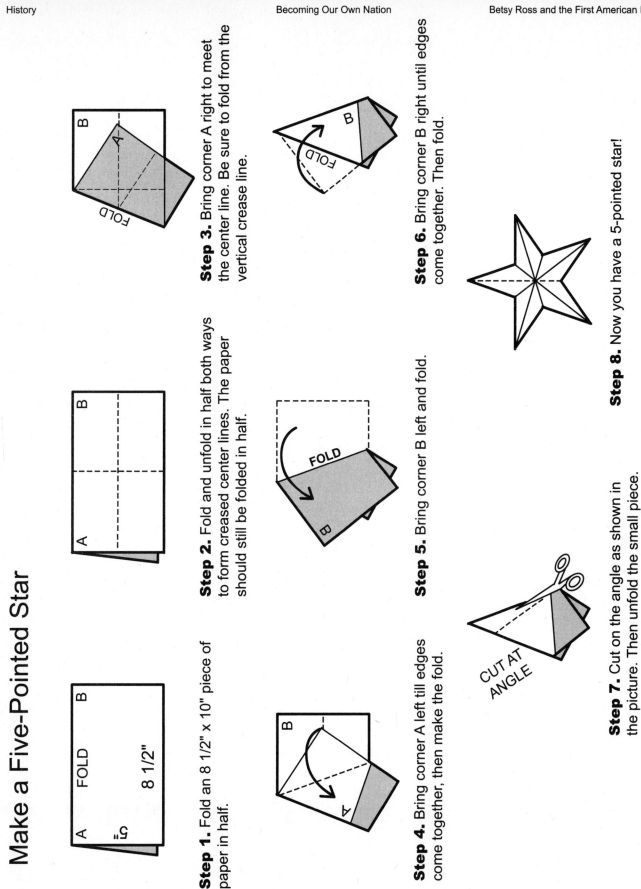

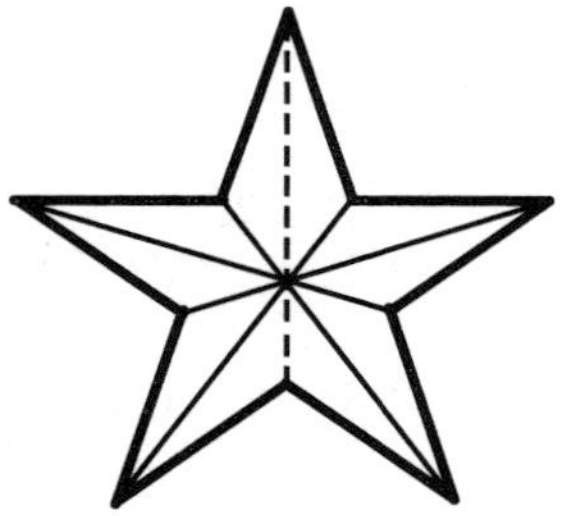

Step 8. Now you have a 5-pointed star!

Name Date

Lesson Assessment

Betsy Ross and the First American Flag

1. What country does this flag stand for?

2. How many stripes are there on the American flag?
3. What do the stripes on the American flag stand for?
4. How many stars does the flag of the United States have today?
5. What does each star on the American flag stand for?
6. What was the name of the woman who sewed the first American flag?

Student Guide
Lesson 3: George Washington

Learn about George Washington, who was the leader of the American army during the Revolutionary War and the first president of the United States of America. Get to know what George Washington was like as a person. A national hero, [NGT]he was also famous for [NGT]his honesty.

Lesson Objectives

- Identify George Washington as the first president of the United States of America.
- Identify George Washington as a person known for his honesty

---

PREPARE

Approximate lesson time is 45 minutes.

Materials

For the Student

dollar

quarter

Optional

paints, finger

paper, colored construction, 12"x12"

stickers, small round red

twig

Elmer's Glue-All

pencils, colored, 16 or more

large, stiff feathers

pen, ballpoint

LEARN

Activity 1: Getting to Know George Washington *(Online)*

Activity 2: The Story of George Washington and the Cherry Tree *(Online)*

Activity 3: General Washington and the Proud Corporal *(Online)*

Activity 4: Creating a Cherry Tree *(Online)*

ASSESS

Lesson Assessment: George Washington (*Online*)

You will complete an offline assessment covering the main objectives of this lesson. Your learning coach will score this assessment.

LEARN

Activity 5. Optional: Quill Pens *(Online)*

Name Date

Lesson Assessment

George Washington

1. Who was the first president of the United States?
2. Why did the American people want George Washington to be president?

Student Guide
Lesson 4: Thomas Jefferson

Thomas Jefferson was the author of the Declaration of Independence, which includes the famous phrase, "All men are created equal." [NGT]He became the third president of the United States. [NGT]His love of learning and [NGT]his respect for others became guiding ideals of the United States.

Lesson Objectives

- Recall that Thomas Jefferson wrote the Declaration of Independence.
- Identify Thomas Jefferson as the third president of the United States.

PREPARE

Approximate lesson time is 45 minutes.

Materials

For the Student

coin - nickel

Optional

Declaration of Independence coloring sheet

crayons, 16 or more

The Fourth of July Story by Alice Dalgliesh

Keywords and Pronunciation

Monticello (mahn-tuh-CHEH-loh)

LEARN

Activity 1: Who Was Thomas Jefferson? *(Online)*

Activity 2: The Boy Who Loved to Learn *(Online)*

Activity 3: Jefferson: Inventor, Writer, President *(Online)*

Activity 4: Jefferson and the Declaration of Independence *(Online)*

Activity 5: Presenting the Declaration of Independence *(Online)*

ASSESS

Lesson Assessment: Thomas Jefferson (*Online*)

You will complete an offline assessment covering the main objectives of this lesson. Your learning coach will score this assessment.

LEARN

Activity 6. Optional: Looking Around Monticello *(Online)*

Activity 7. Optional: Your Fourth of July Story *(Online)*

Thomas Jefferson Presents the Declaration of Independence

Name Date

Lesson Assessment

Thomas Jefferson

1. Who wrote the Declaration of Independence?

2. Who was the third president of the United States?

Student Guide
Lesson 1: Johnny Appleseed

Meet some of the real and imaginary heroes of early America. Trek westward across the United States with Johnny Appleseed, Sacagawea, Lewis, and Clark. Then meet the incredible Paul Bunyan, and learn about Sequoyah--inventor of the Cherokee written language.

John Chapman was an American pioneer who traveled west from Massachusetts to Indiana. He spent his life planting and tending apple trees and has earned legendary status as "Johnny Appleseed."

Lesson Objectives

- Explain that when the United States was new, many people moved westward.
- Identify Johnny Appleseed as a man who traveled westward planting apple trees along his way.
- Name the American Revolution as the war in which the United States won its independence from England.
- Identify George Washington as the first president of the United States of America.
- Identify Thomas Jefferson as the third president of the United States.

PREPARE

Approximate lesson time is 45 minutes.

Materials

For the Student

- map of United States
- map marker, world and U.S.
- map, U.S.

Optional

- Johnny Appleseed coloring sheet
- crayons, 16 or more
- Johnny Appleseed by Reeve Lindbergh

LEARN

Activity 1: Reviewing United States History *(Online)*

Activity 2: Getting to Know Johnny Appleseed *(Online)*

Activity 3: Tale of Johnny Appleseed *(Online)*

Activity 4: Johnny's Journey *(Offline)*

Activity 5. Optional: Making Johnny Appleseed Come Alive *(Offline)*

ASSESS

Lesson Assessment: Johnny Appleseed (*Online*)

You will complete an offline assessment covering the main objectives of this lesson. Your learning coach will score this assessment.

LEARN

Activity 6. Optional: Reading About Johnny Appleseed *(Offline)*

United States of America

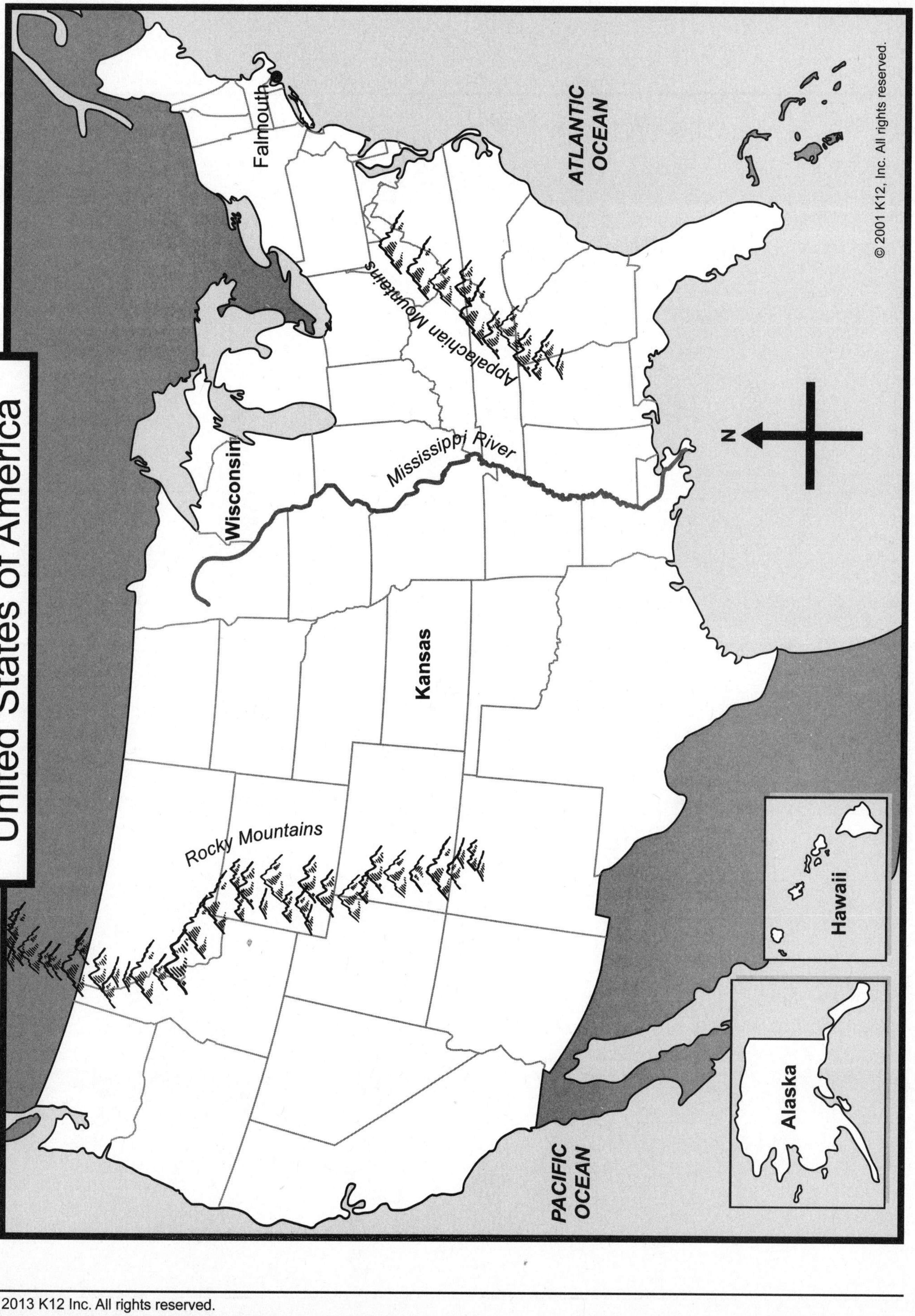

Johnny Appleseed

Name Date

Lesson Assessment

Johnny Appleseed

1. When the United States was new, what were many people doing?

2. Who was Johnny Appleseed?

Student Guide
Lesson 2: Lewis and Clark and Sacagawea

Lesson Objectives

- Recognize the four cardinal directions: north, south, east, and west.
- Locate the Appalachians, Rocky Mountains, and Mississippi River on a map of the United States.
- Recall that Thomas Jefferson wrote the Declaration of Independence.
- Define pioneer as an early settler of the American West.
- Locate the Rocky Mountains on a map.
- Locate the Pacific Ocean on a map.
- Name Sacagawea as a young Shoshone woman who helped Lewis and Clark during their journey.
- Name Lewis and Clark as leaders of an important voyage of exploration in the American West.
- Locate the Mississippi River on a map.

PREPARE

Approximate lesson time is 45 minutes.

Materials

For the Student

map of the Louisiana Purchase

map, U.S.

Optional

Sacagawea: The Journey to the West by Nora Kroeber

Keywords and Pronunciation

Sacagawea (sak-uh-juh-WEE-uh)
Shoshone (shuh-SHOH-nee)

LEARN

Activity 1: Look at the United States *(Online)*

Activity 2: Looking West *(Online)*

Activity 3: A Poem *(Online)*

ASSESS

Lesson Assessment: Lewis and Clark and Sacagawea (*Online*)

You will complete an offline assessment covering the main objectives of this lesson. Your learning coach will score this assessment.

LEARN

Activity 4. Optional: Read Aloud *(Offline)*

Louisiana Purchase

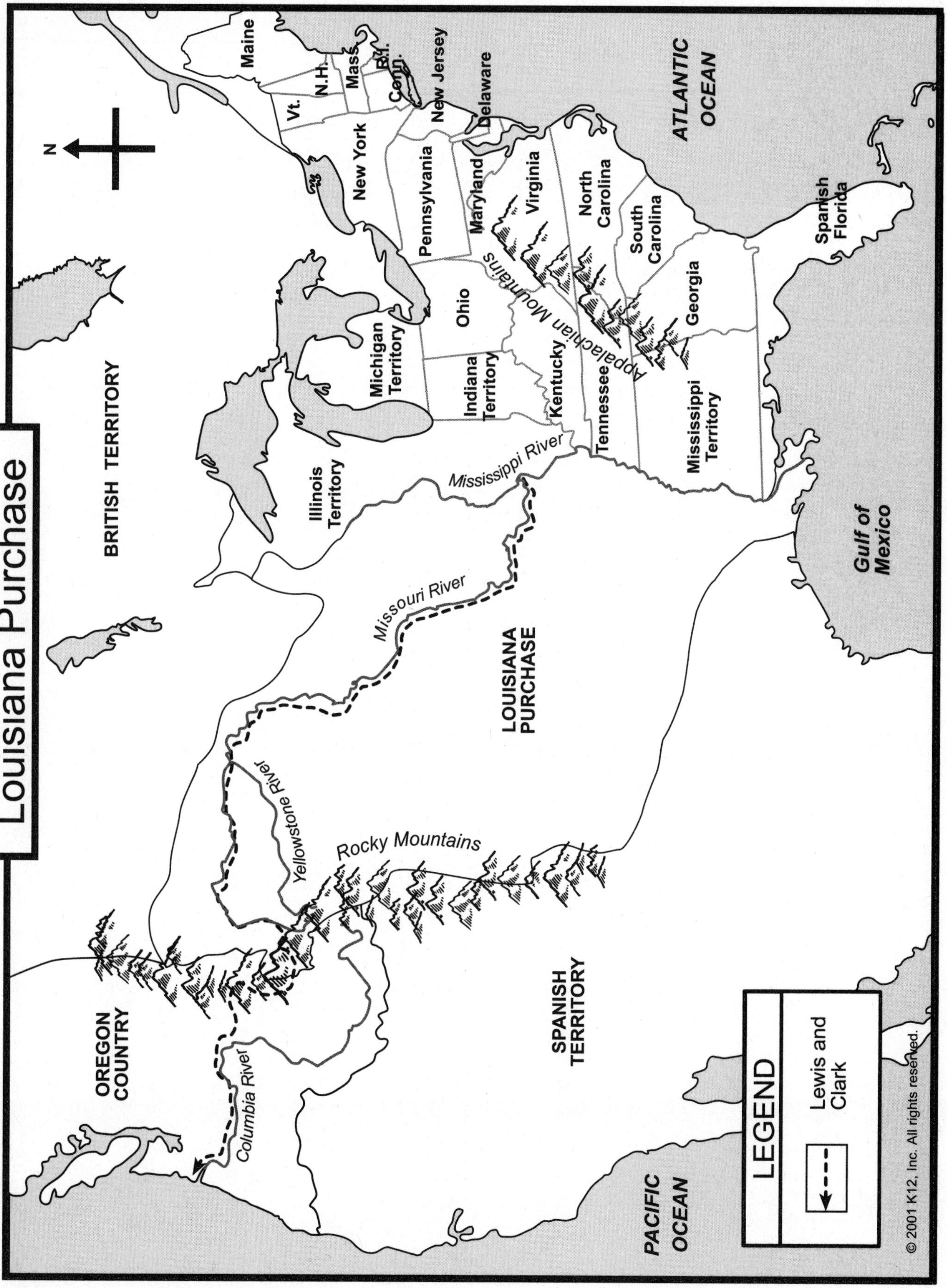

N
BRITISH TERRITORY
Maine
N.H.
Vt.
Mass.
R.I.
Conn.
New York
New Jersey
Delaware
Pennsylvania
Maryland
Virginia
North Carolina
South Carolina
Georgia
Ohio
Michigan Territory
Indiana Territory
Kentucky
Tennessee
Mississippi Territory
Illinois Territory
Spanish Florida
Appalachian Mountains
ATLANTIC OCEAN
Gulf of Mexico
Mississippi River
Missouri River
LOUISIANA PURCHASE
Yellowstone River
Rocky Mountains
OREGON COUNTRY
Columbia River
SPANISH TERRITORY
PACIFIC OCEAN
LEGEND
Lewis and Clark
© 2001 K12, Inc. All rights reserved.

Name Date

Lesson Assessment

Lewis and Clark and Sacagawea

1. What are the names of the two men who led a voyage of exploration in the American West?
2. What is the name of the Shoshone girl who helped Lewis and Clark on their expedition?
3. In order to answer this question you will need to use the map of the US. Where is the the Mississippi River?
4. In order to answer this question you will need to use the map of the US. Where are the the Rocky Mountains?
5. In order to answer this question you will need to use the map of the US. Where is the the Pacific Ocean?

Student Guide
Lesson 3: Paul Bunyan

As pioneers traveled west, they built homes and towns, and they told tall tales. Today we hear about a legendary lumberjack named Paul Bunyan and his friend Babe the Blue Ox.

Lesson Objectives

- Identify Paul Bunyan as a legendary lumberjack.
- Define a tall tale as an exaggerated, make-believe story.
- Know that pioneers kept traveling west, all the way to California.
- Recognize the four cardinal directions: north, south, east, and west.
- Identify Johnny Appleseed as a man who traveled westward planting apple trees along his way.
- Name Lewis and Clark as leaders of an important voyage of exploration in the American West.

PREPARE

Approximate lesson time is 45 minutes.

Materials

For the Student

map, U.S.

map of the United States

Optional

Paul Bunyan and Babe coloring sheet

crayons, 16 or more

Paul Bunyan by Steven Kellogg

Paul Bunyan, narrated by Jonathan Winters

Pecos Bill by Steven Kellogg

Sally Ann Thunder Ann Whirlwind Crockett: A Tall Tale by Steven Kellogg

---

LEARN
Activity 1: Traveling West *(Online)*

Activity 2: Go West! *(Online)*

Activity 3: Paul Bunyan *(Online)*

Activity 4. Optional: The Adventures of Paul and Babe *(Offline)*

ASSESS

Lesson Assessment: Paul Bunyan (*Online*)

Consider what your student learned during the lesson. Was he able to locate a place, identify a person, recall an event, or otherwise show that he achieved the objectives? Answer the following questions based on your observations.

LEARN

Activity 5. Optional: Read About Paul Bunyan *(Offline)*

United States of America

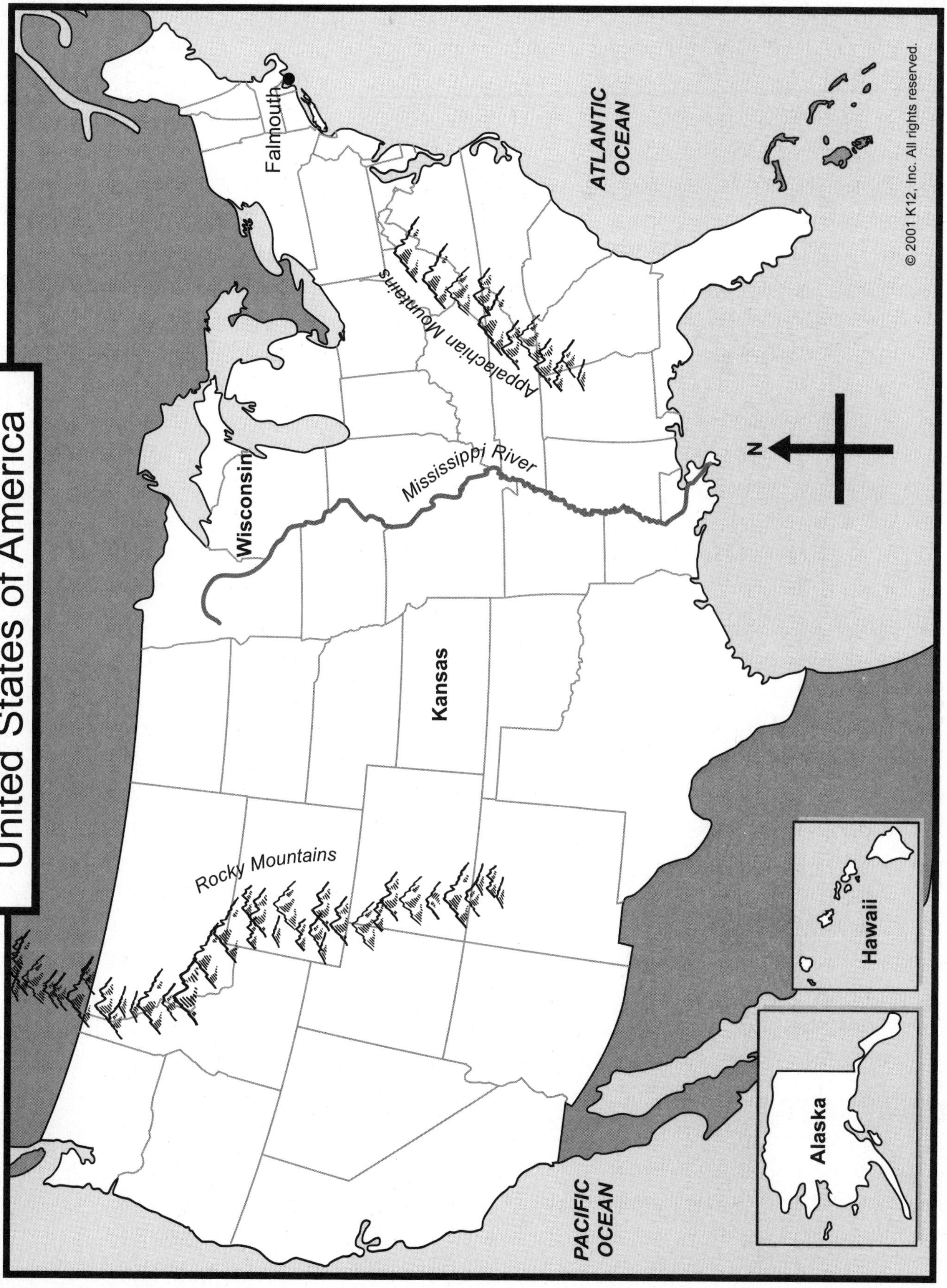

Paul Bunyan and Babe the Blue Ox

Name Date

Lesson Assessment

Paul Bunyan

1. Who was Paul Bunyan?

2. What is a tall tale?

3. How far west did pioneers travel?

Student Guide
Lesson 4: Sequoyah's Great Invention

The Cherokee did not have a way to write their language until the early 1800s when Sequoya, with single-minded dedication, invented a writing system for the Cherokee language.

Lesson Objectives

- Identify the Anasazi as an American Indian tribe who once inhabited the American Southwest.
- Identify the Plains Indians as hunters of buffalo.
- Explain that the Abenaki relied on and made good use of the plant and animal resources in the Eastern Woodlands for their food, homes, clothing, and more.
- Identify Sequoyah as the Cherokee Indian who invented a way of writing the Cherokee language.
- Describe the importance of writing.

PREPARE

Approximate lesson time is 45 minutes.

Materials

For the Student
- map of First Americans

Optional
- Sequoyah and Ayoka coloring sheet
- crayons, 16 or more
- pencils, no. 2

Keywords and Pronunciation

Ayoka (ay-OH-kuh)
Cherokee (CHER-uh-kee)
Sequoyah (sih-KWOY-uh)

LEARN

Activity 1: Learn About the Cherokee *(Online)*

Activity 2: The Beginning of Cherokee Writing *(Online)*

Activity 3: Sequoyah Invents the Cherokee Alphabet *(Online)*

Activity 4. Optional: Writing Like Sequoyah *(Offline)*

Activity 5: Betsy's Flag *(Online)*

Help Betsy Ross complete the first American flag by correctly identifying some of the people introduced in units 11, 12, and 13. Click Student Activity to get started.

ASSESS

Lesson Assessment: Sequoyah's Great Invention (*Online*)

You will complete an offline assessment covering the main objectives of this lesson. Your learning coach will score this assessment.

LEARN

Activity 6. Optional: Giant Trees *(Online)*

First Americans

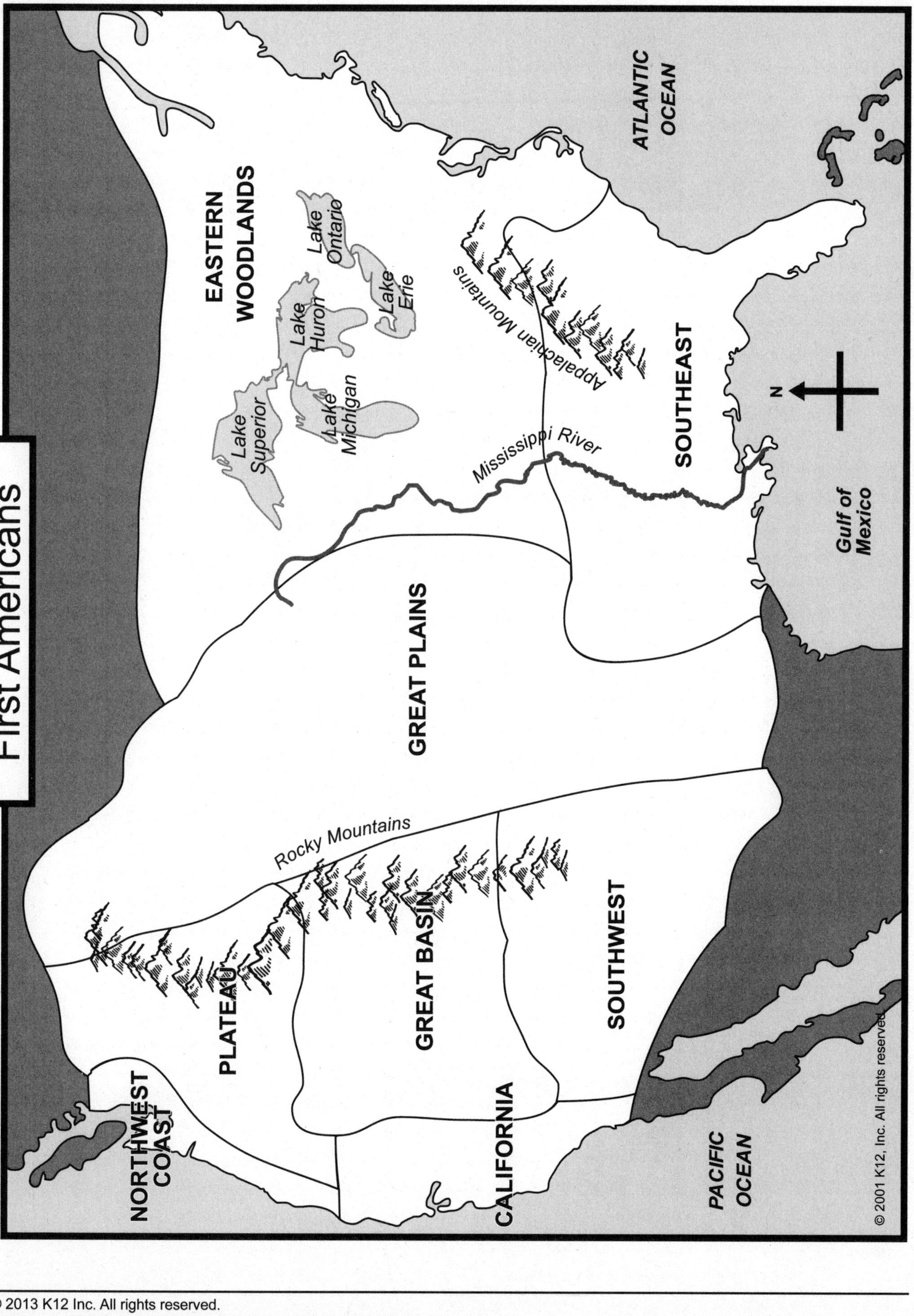

EASTERN WOODLANDS
Lake Superior
Lake Michigan
Lake Huron
Lake Ontario
Lake Erie
Appalachian Mountains
ATLANTIC OCEAN
SOUTHEAST
Mississippi River
N
Gulf of Mexico
GREAT PLAINS
Rocky Mountains
PLATEAU
GREAT BASIN
SOUTHWEST
NORTHWEST COAST
CALIFORNIA
PACIFIC OCEAN
© 2001 K12, Inc. All rights reserved.

Sequoyah and Ayoka
ᎬᏺᏧᏻ ᏙᏃᎠᎾ ᎠᏫᏗ ᎥᏃᏙᏌᎠ

Name Date

Lesson Assessment

Sequoyah's Great Invention

1. Why is writing important?
2. Who was Sequoyah?

Student Guide
Lesson 1: Thomas Hopkins Gallaudet

As the United States grew and changed, many different people led the nation forward. Some helped end the terrible evil of slavery; others worked for betterment in different ways. Learn how Thomas Hopkins Gallaudet, Harriet Tubman, Abraham Lincoln, and Susan B. Anthony helped both individuals and their country.

When Thomas Hopkins Gallaudet met nine-year-old Alice Cogswell, he realized that deaf people could learn how to read and write. He traveled to France to learn how to teach deaf children. When he returned, he founded the first American School for the Deaf.

Lesson Objectives

- Identify Sequoyah as the Cherokee Indian who invented a way of writing the Cherokee language.
- Explain that a deaf person cannot hear.
- Identify Thomas Hopkins Gallaudet as the person who started the first American school for deaf children.
- Explain that many deaf people use American Sign Language to communicate.

PREPARE

Approximate lesson time is 45 minutes.

Materials

For the Student

globe, inflatable

ASL Alphabet sheet

ASL Words and Phrases sheet

Keywords and Pronunciation

Laurent Clerc (lor-AHN kler)

Thomas Hopkins Gallaudet (gal-uh-DET)

LEARN

Activity 1: Getting Started *(Online)*

Activity 2: Thomas Gallaudet Meets Alice *(Online)*

Activity 3: Gallaudet's Voyage *(Online)*

Activity 4: American Sign Language Dialogue *(Online)*

ASSESS

Lesson Assessment: Thomas Hopkins Gallaudet (*Online*)

You will complete an offline assessment covering the main objectives of this lesson. Your learning coach will score this assessment.

American Sign Language Alphabet

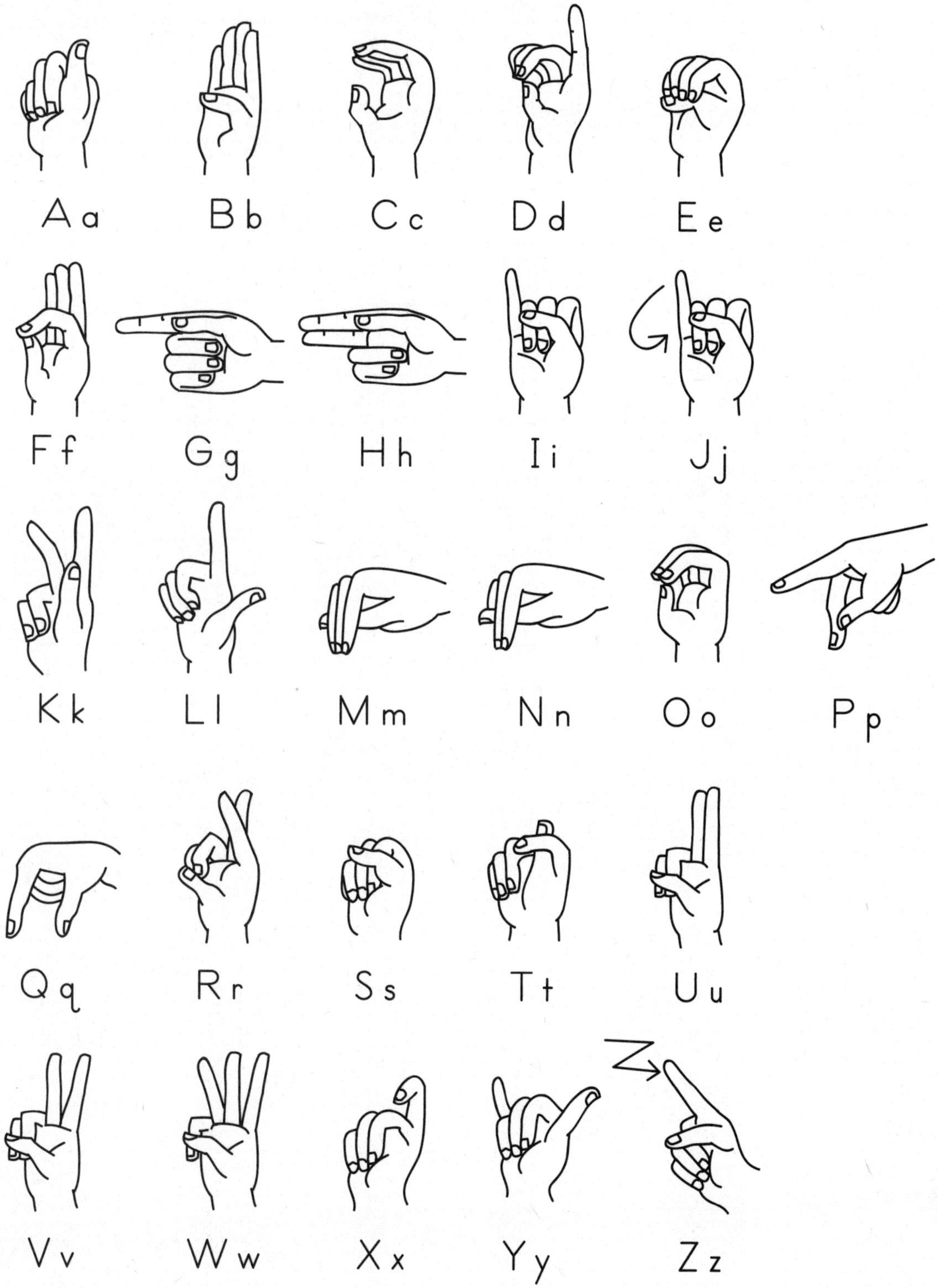

American Sign Language Words and Phrases

Hi

My name is

American Sign Language Words and Phrases

Your

name

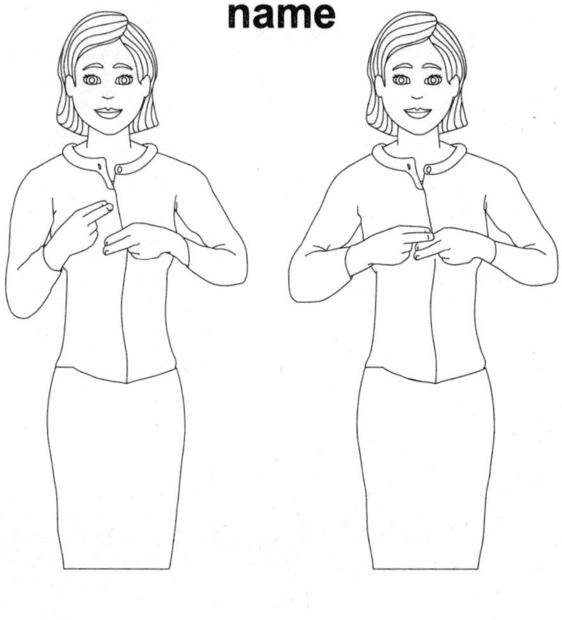

what

Name Date

Lesson Assessment

Thomas Hopkins Gallaudet

1. What is it that a deaf person cannot do?

2. Who started the first American school for deaf children?

3. What language do many American deaf people use to communicate?

Student Guide

Lesson 2: Harriet Tubman and the Underground Railroad

Lesson Objectives

- Identify Harriet Tubman as a woman who escaped from slavery and helped others do the same.
- Describe how slaves traveled north by following the stars of the Drinking Gourd (or Big Dipper) to freedom.
- Explain that the Underground Railroad was not a real railroad but a way for slaves to get to the North and become free.

PREPARE

Approximate lesson time is 45 minutes.

Materials

For the Student

- Follow the Drinking Gourd discussion sheet
- Follow the Drinking Gourd by Jeannette Winter (ISBN 0679819975)
- map of the Underground Railroad
- Big Dipper coloring sheet
- crayons, 16 or more
- paper, colored construction, 12"x12"
- pencils, no. 2
- stickers - silver stars

LEARN

Activity 1: Review *(Online)*

Activity 2: The Drinking Gourd *(Online)*

Activity 3: Read Aloud *(Offline)*

Activity 4: Underground Railroad Map *(Offline)*

Activity 5: Follow the Drinking Gourd *(Offline)*

Activity 6: Big Dipper *(Online)*

ASSESS

Lesson Assessment: Harriet Tubman and the Underground Railroad (*Online*)

You will complete an offline assessment covering the main objectives of this lesson. Your learning coach will score this assessment.

LEARN

Activity 7. Optional: The Drinking Gourd Constellation *(Offline)*

Follow the Drinking Gourd Discussion Questions

After reading page 3, explain that a plantation is a big farm.

After reading page 5, ask the question:

What drinking gourd do you think Joe is talking about?

the stars or the Big Dipper

After reading page 16, ask the student to find Joe's mark on the tree.

After reading page 29, ask the questions:

Is the Underground Railroad a train? What was the Underground Railroad?

The Underground Railroad is not a train. It's the name of the network Harriet Tubman and others developed to move slaves from the South to freedom in the North.

What is the name of the woman who escaped from slavery and helped others do the same?

Harriet Tubman

How did escaping slaves know they were traveling north?

They followed the stars of the Drinking Gourd, or Big Dipper.

Underground Railroad Routes, 1860

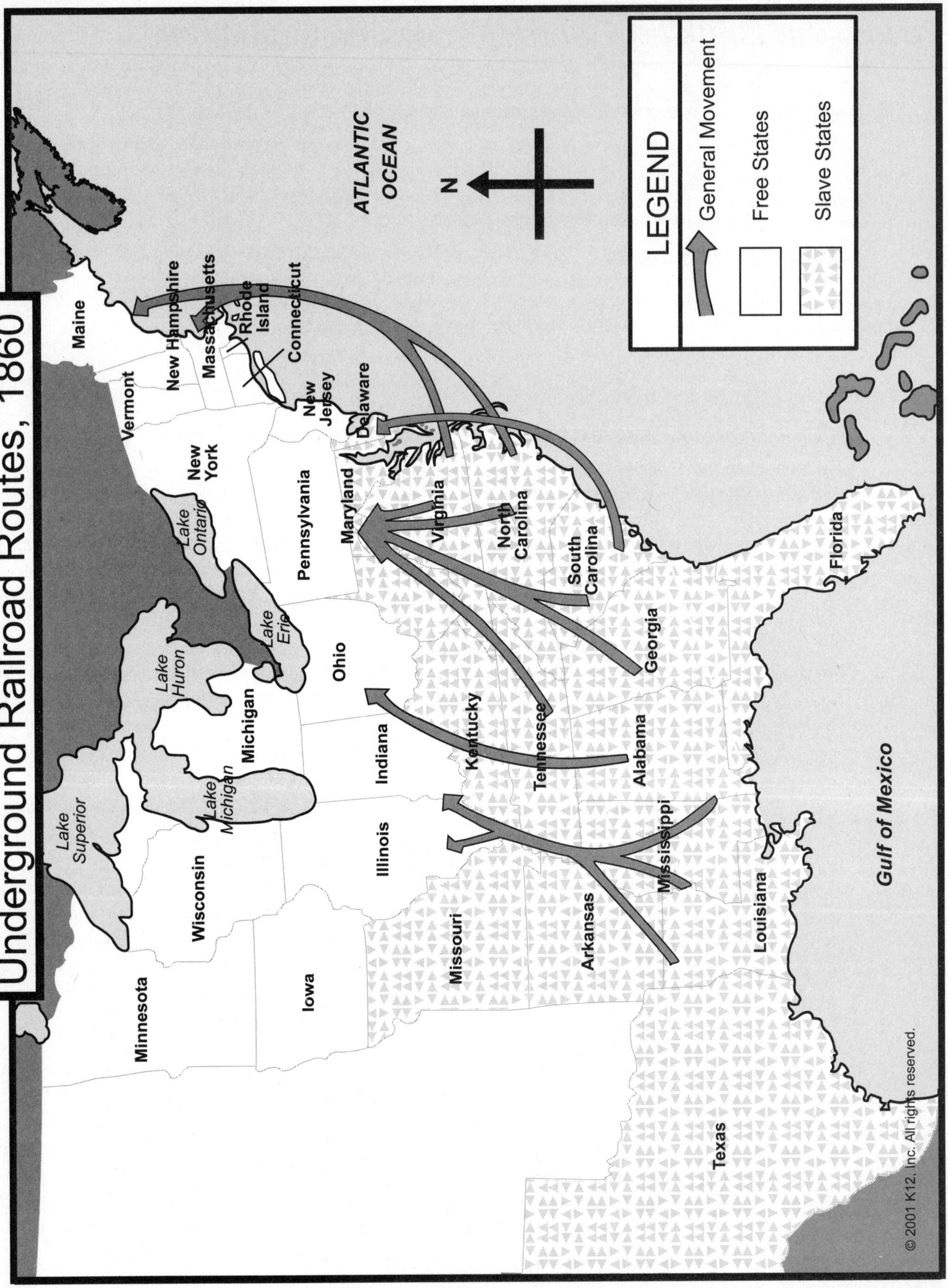
Maine
New Hampshire
Vermont
Massachusetts
Rhode Island
Connecticut
New York
New Jersey
Delaware
Pennsylvania
Maryland
Virginia
North Carolina
South Carolina
Georgia
Florida
Ohio
Michigan
Indiana
Illinois
Kentucky
Tennessee
Alabama
Mississippi
Wisconsin
Minnesota
Iowa
Missouri
Arkansas
Louisiana
Texas
Lake Superior
Lake Michigan
Lake Huron
Lake Erie
Lake Ontario
ATLANTIC OCEAN
N
Gulf of Mexico
LEGEND
General Movement
Free States
Slave States
© 2001 K12. Inc. All rights reserved.

Name Date

Lesson Assessment

Harriet Tubman and the Underground Railroad

1. What is the name of the woman who escaped from slavery and helped others do the same?

2. How did escaping slaves know they were traveling north?

3. What was the Underground Railroad?

Student Guide
Lesson 3: "Honest Abe": Abraham Lincoln

From humble beginnings in a log cabin, Abraham Lincoln became one of the greatest presidents of the United States. Renowned for his plainspoken eloquence and integrity, he became known as "Honest Abe." He strongly opposed slavery and held the United States together during the Civil War.

Lesson Objectives

- Identify Harriet Tubman as a woman who escaped from slavery and helped others do the same.
- Describe how slaves traveled north by following the stars of the Drinking Gourd (or Big Dipper) to freedom.
- Explain that the Underground Railroad was not a real railroad but a way for slaves to get to the North and become free.
- Explain that Abraham Lincoln became a president of the United States.
- Explain that Lincoln believed slavery was wrong.
- Explain that Abraham Lincoln grew up as a pioneer.
- Describe Lincoln as a man known for his honesty.
- Identify the Lincoln Memorial.

PREPARE

Approximate lesson time is 45 minutes.

Materials

For the Student

map of the United States, 1863

crayons, 16 or more

Optional

paper, colored construction, 12"x12"

pencils, colored, 16 or more

tape, clear

Abe Lincoln's Life Pictures

Abe Lincoln's Hat by Martha Brenner

LEARN

Activity 1: Reviewing the State of Slavery *(Online)*

Activity 2: Abraham Lincoln *(Online)*

Activity 3: Abraham Lincoln Fights Slavery *(Online)*

Activity 4. Optional: Make a Stovepipe Hat *(Offline)*

Activity 5. Optional: Abe Lincoln's Life *(Offline)*

ASSESS

Lesson Assessment: "Honest Abe": Abraham Lincoln (*Online*)

You will complete an offline assessment covering the main objectives of this lesson. Your learning coach will score this assessment.

LEARN

Activity 6. Optional: Learn More About Abraham Lincoln *(Offline)*

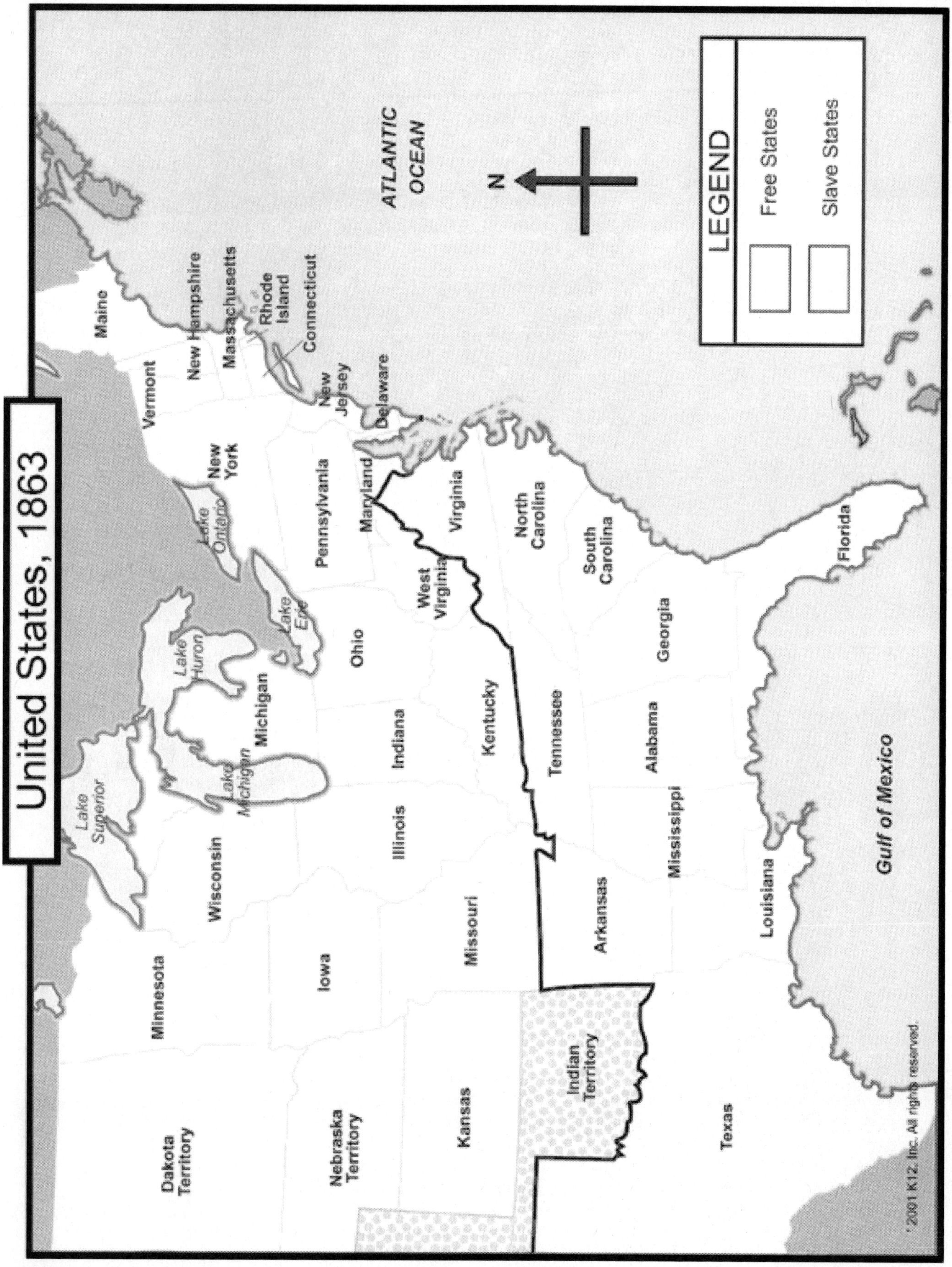
United States, 1863
Lake Superior
Lake Michigan
Lake Huron
Lake Ontario
Lake Erie
Maine
Vermont
New Hampshire
Massachusetts
Rhode Island
Connecticut
New York
New Jersey
Delaware
Pennsylvania
Maryland
Michigan
Ohio
West Virginia
Virginia
North Carolina
South Carolina
Georgia
Florida
Wisconsin
Indiana
Kentucky
Tennessee
Alabama
Illinois
Mississippi
Minnesota
Iowa
Missouri
Arkansas
Louisiana
Dakota Territory
Nebraska Territory
Kansas
Indian Territory
Texas
ATLANTIC OCEAN
Gulf of Mexico
N
LEGEND
Free States
Slave States
© 2001 K12, Inc. All rights reserved.

Name Date

Lesson Assessment

"Honest Abe": Abraham Lincoln

1. What do we call people who traveled to the west and built their homes in the wilderness like Abraham Lincoln and his family?
2. What did Abraham Lincoln become?
3. What was Abraham Lincoln known for?
4. What did Abraham Lincoln believe about slavery?
5. In order to answer this question, please use a standard U.S.A. penny. What is shown on the back of the penny?

Student Guide
Lesson 4: Susan B. Anthony: Women's Rights

Susan B. Anthony campaigned tirelessly to earn equal rights for women and women's right to vote. Fourteen years after her death, Congress passed the 19th Amendment, granting women the right to vote.

Lesson Objectives

- Describe Lincoln as a man known for his honesty.
- Explain that Lincoln believed slavery was wrong.
- Identify Susan B. Anthony as a woman who worked for women's rights.
- Tell that Susan B. Anthony worked hard to get women the right to vote.

PREPARE

Approximate lesson time is 45 minutes.

Materials

For the Student

penny

Susan B. Anthony coloring sheet

crayons, 16 or more

Optional

pencils, no. 2

paper, 8 1/2" x 11"

Bloomers by Rhoda Blumberg

LEARN

Activity 1: Remember Honest Abe *(Online)*

Activity 2: Susan B. Anthony *(Online)*

Activity 3: Susan B. Anthony Coloring Activity *(Offline)*

Activity 4. Optional: Thank You, Susan B. Anthony *(Offline)*

ASSESS

Lesson Assessment: Susan B. Anthony: Women's Rights (*Online*)

You will complete an offline assessment covering the main objectives of this lesson. Your learning coach will score this assessment.

LEARN

Activity 5. Optional: Bloomers *(Offline)*

Susan B. Anthony worked hard for women's rights.

Name Date

Lesson Assessment

Susan B. Anthony: Women's Rights

1. Who worked for women's rights?

2. Who worked hard to get women the right to vote?

Student Guide
Lesson 1: Laura Ingalls Wilder

After the Civil War, America was in motion. Railroads connected the country, pioneers went west, and immigrants came from around the world. Hear the stories of John Henry, Laura Ingalls Wilder, and immigrants who were greeted by the Statue of Liberty.

Laura Ingalls Wilder grew up as a pioneer girl on the prairies of the Midwest. As an adult she wrote down the stories from her life in the "Little House" books, immortalizing the hardy pioneers' struggle to settle the West.

Lesson Objectives

- Identify Johnny Appleseed as a man who traveled westward planting apple trees along his way.
- Name Lewis and Clark as leaders of an important voyage of exploration in the American West.
- Describe Laura Ingalls Wilder as a pioneer who grew up to become an author.
- Define pioneer as an early settler of the American West.

PREPARE

Approximate lesson time is 45 minutes.

Materials

For the Student

- map of the United States

Optional

- Covered Wagon activity sheet
- Pioneering with Laura activity sheet
- crayons, 16 or more
- pencils, no. 2
- Laura Ingalls Wilder by Ginger Wadsworth
- Little House in the Big Woods by Laura Ingalls Wilder

Keywords and Pronunciation

Osage (oh-SAYJ)

pioneers : A group of people who are the first to settle in a new place or territory.

LEARN

Activity 1: American History Review *(Online)*

Activity 2: Pioneers Go West *(Online)*

Activity 3. Optional: Pioneering with Laura *(Offline)*

Activity 4. Optional: What Would You Take? *(Offline)*

ASSESS

Lesson Test: Laura Ingalls Wilder (*Online*)

You will complete an offline assessment covering the main objectives of this lesson. Your learning coach will score this assessment.

LEARN

Activity 5. Optional: Laura's Little House *(Offline)*

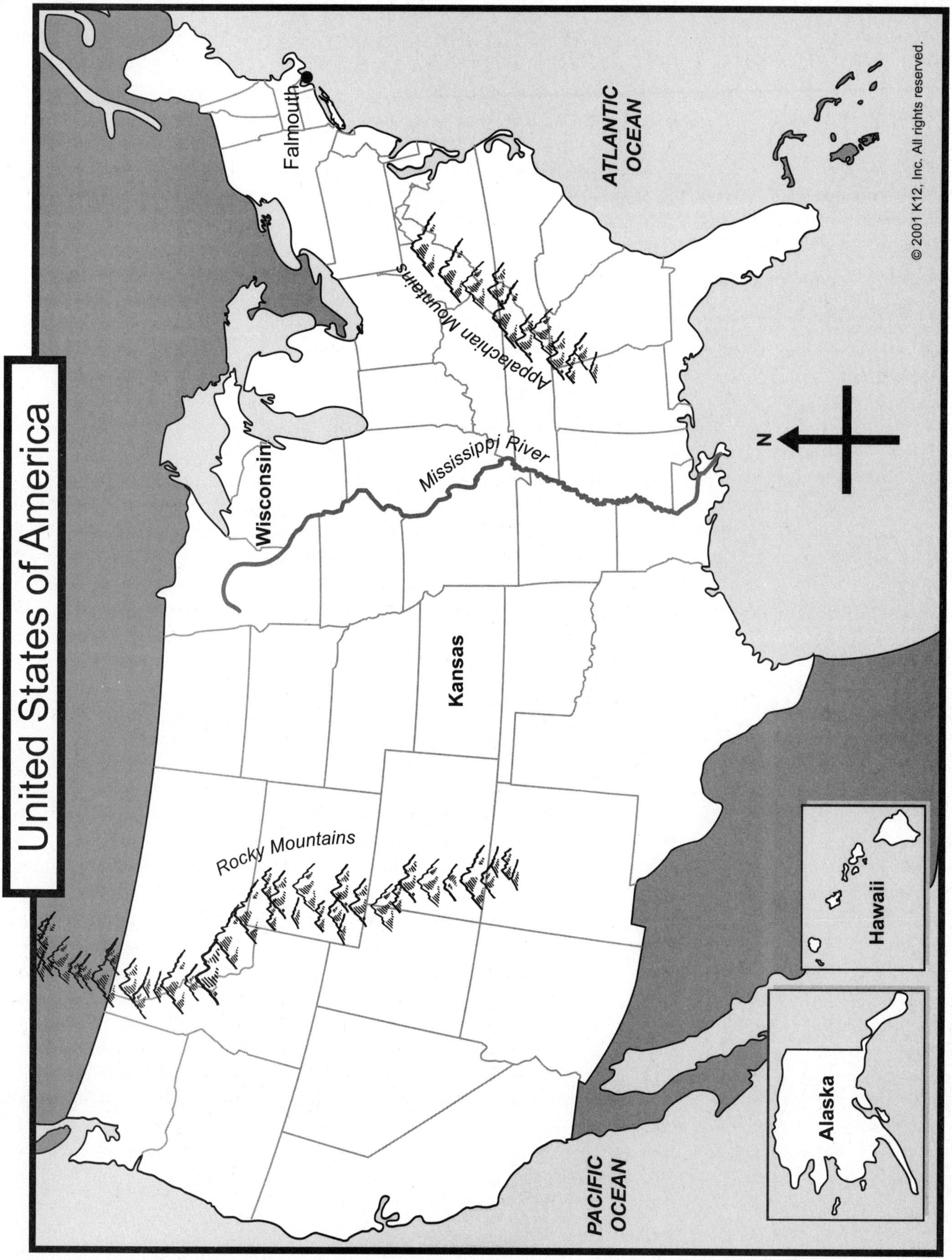
United States of America
Falmouth
ATLANTIC OCEAN
Appalachian Mountains
Mississippi River
Wisconsin
Kansas
Rocky Mountains
PACIFIC OCEAN
Hawaii
Alaska
N
© 2001 K12, Inc. All rights reserved.

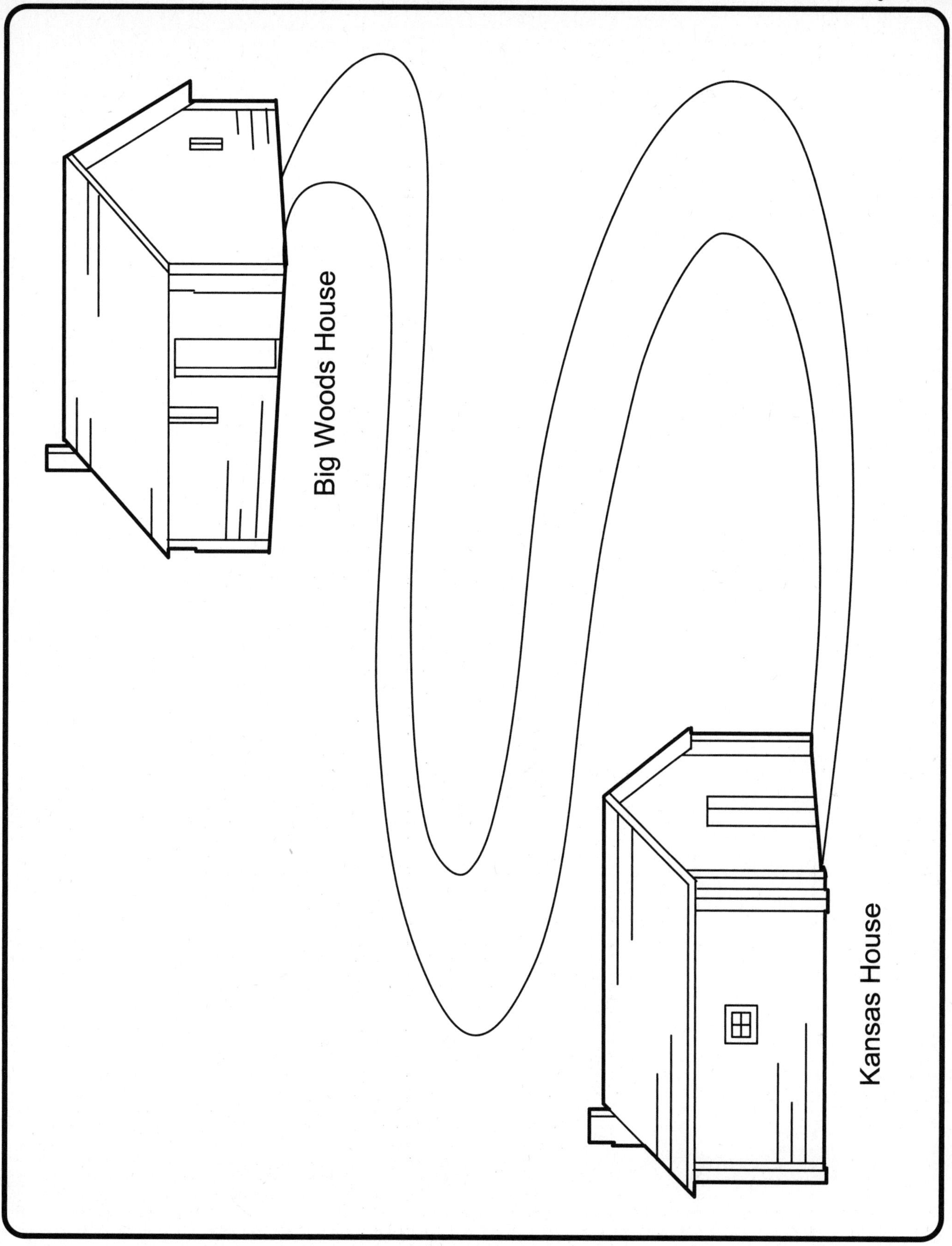
Big Woods House
Kansas House

Name Date

Lesson Assessment

Laura Ingalls Wilder

1. Explain who the pioneers were.
2. Who was Laura Ingalls Wilder?
3. Why were Laura and her family considered pioneers?

Student Guide

Lesson 2: John Henry and the Railroad

Around the time of the Civil War, railroads became important to the growth of the United States. Men worked ceaselessly to lay track, and many legends grew up around them. One man, John Henry, was known for his determination and strength, and he is still remembered in legend and song.

Lesson Objectives

- Define pioneer as an early settler of the American West.
- Identify John Henry as a strong, determined railroad worker who battled a machine.
- Locate the Atlantic and Pacific Oceans, the Appalachians, the Mississippi River, and the Rocky Mountains on a map of the United States.

PREPARE

Approximate lesson time is 45 minutes.

Materials

For the Student

- map of the United States
- globe, inflatable
- Working on the Railroad song sheet

Optional

- Train activity sheet
- paper, heavy
- crayons, 16 or more
- Elmer's Glue-All
- popsicle sticks
- scissors, round-end safety
- tape, clear
- The Legend of John Henry coloring sheet
- John Henry and His Mighty Hammer by Patsy Jensen
- John Henry by Julius Lester
- John Henry: An American Legend by Ezra Jack Keats

LEARN

Activity 1: Oceans and Mountains *(Online)*

Activity 2: The Railroads *(Online)*

Activity 3: Song: I've Been Working on the Railroad *(Offline)*

Activity 4: John Henry *(Online)*

Activity 5: Song: John Henry *(Offline)*

Activity 6. Optional: Trains on the Move *(Offline)*

Activity 7. Optional: The Legend of John Henry *(Offline)*

ASSESS

Lesson Assessment: John Henry and the Railroad (*Online*)

You will complete an offline assessment covering the main objectives of this lesson. Your learning coach will score this assessment.

LEARN

Activity 8. Optional: Reading About John Henry *(Offline)*

United States of America

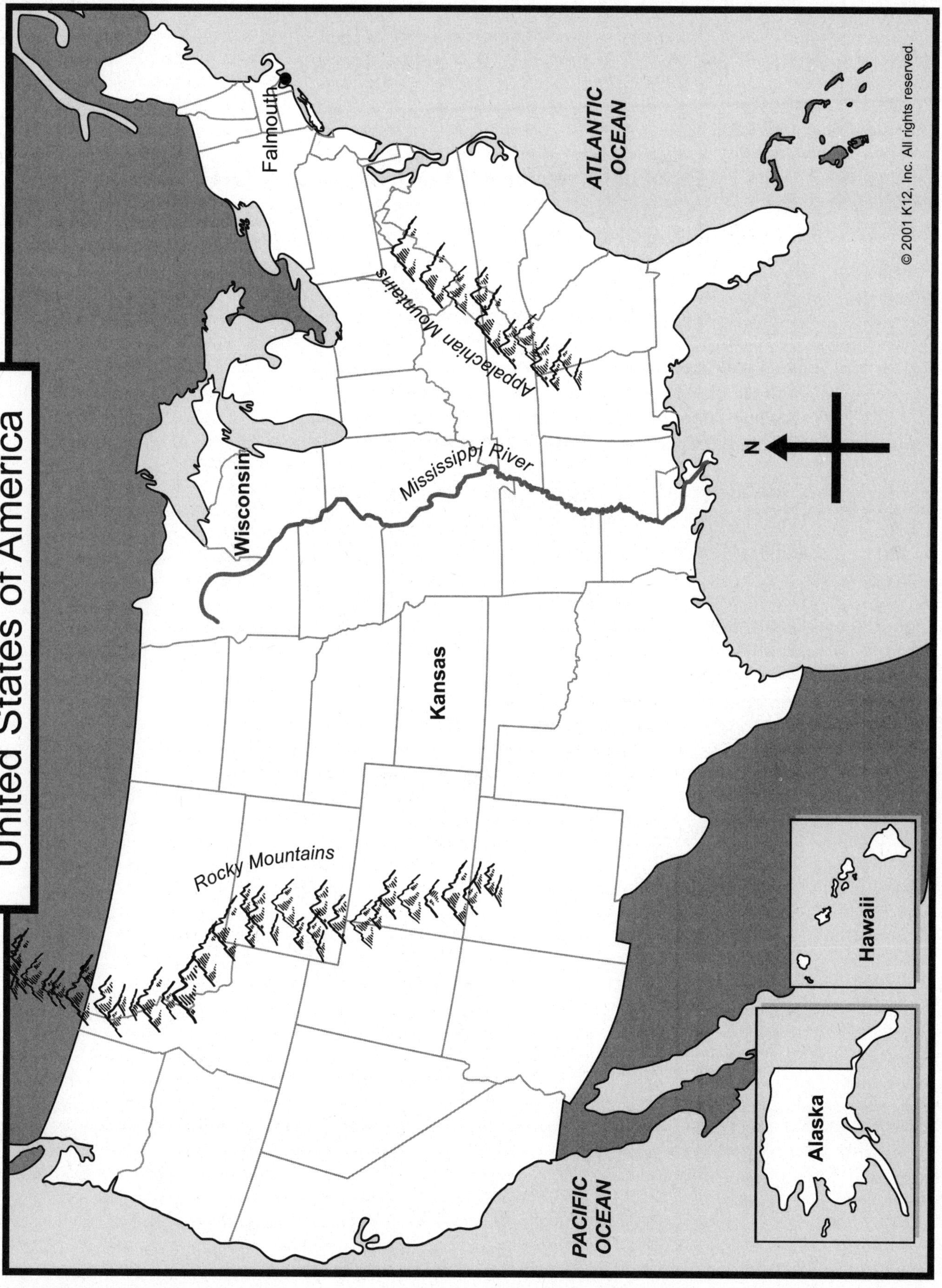

I've Been Working on the Railroad

I've been working on the railroad, *(swing imaginary sledgehammer with both hands)*
All the livelong day. *(wipe hand across forehead)*
I've been working on the railroad, *(swing hammer)*
Just to pass the time away. *(swing hammer)*

Don't you hear the whistle blowing? *(cup one ear)*
Rise up so early in the morn. *(yawn and stretch)*
Don't you hear the captain shouting, *(cup one ear)*
"Dinah, blow your horn"? *(point and shake finger)*

Dinah, won't you blow, *(blow imaginary horn to the left)*
Dinah, won't you blow, *(blow imaginary horn to the right)*
Dinah, won't you blow your horn? *(blow horn in a circle)*

Dinah, won't you blow, *(blow imaginary horn to the left)*
Dinah, won't you blow, *(blow imaginary horn to the right)*
Dinah, won't you blow your horn? *(blow horn in a circle)*

Someone's in the kitchen with Dinah,
Someone's in the kitchen I know.
Someone's in the kitchen with Dinah,
Strummin' on the old banjo, and singing— *(strum imaginary banjo)*

Fee, fi, fiddly-i-oh,
Fee, fi, fiddly-i-oh,
Fee, fi, fiddly-i-oh,
Strummin' on the old banjo.

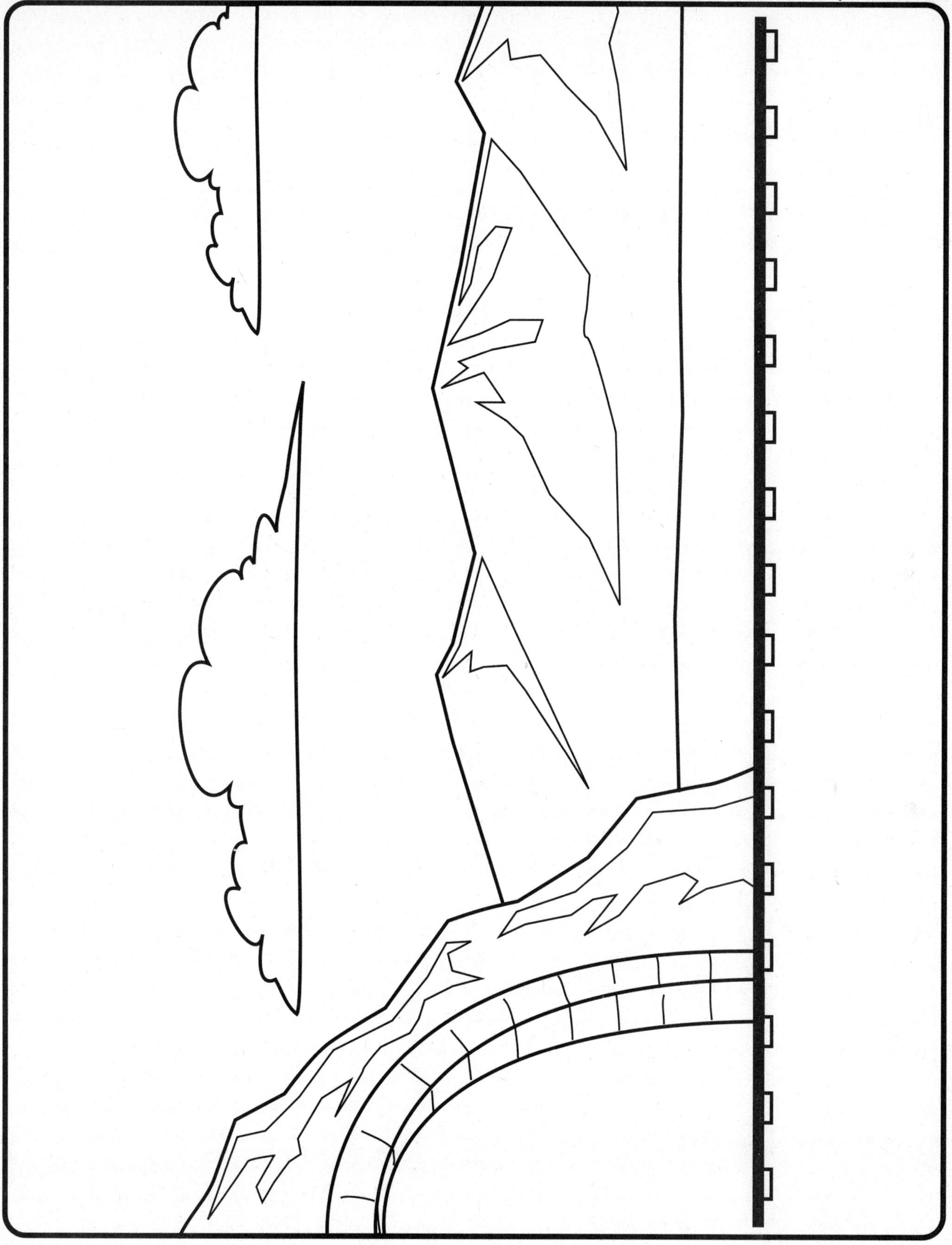

cut

JOHN HENRY

Name Date

Lesson Assessment

John Henry and the Railroad

1. Who was the large man people said was born with a hammer in his hand?
2. What was John Henry's job when he grew up?
3. Describe John Henry.
4. What happened when John Henry battled the steam drill?

Student Guide
Lesson 3: The Statue of Liberty

A gift from France to the United States, the Statue of Liberty has stood for over a hundred years in the New York harbor to welcome millions of immigrants to America.

Lesson Objectives

- Define an immigrant as a person who leaves one country to live in another.
- Tell that the Statue of Liberty was a gift from France to the United States.
- Tell that the Statue of Liberty welcomed immigrants to America.

PREPARE

Approximate lesson time is 45 minutes.

Materials

For the Student
- globe, inflatable

Optional
- Liberty Torch pattern
- paper, colored construction, 12"x12"
- tissue paper
- toilet paper tubes
- Elmer's Glue-All
- glitter
- scissors, round-end safety
- tape, clear
- Welcome to America coloring sheet
- crayons, 16 or more
- The Story of the Statue of Liberty by Betsy Maestro

Keywords and Pronunciation

immigrant (IH muh gruhnt) : A person who leaves one country to settle permanently in another.

LEARN

Activity 1: America the Beautiful *(Online)*

Activity 2: Bridget Meets Lady Liberty *(Online)*

Activity 3: Irving Berlin: God Bless America *(Online)*

Activity 4. Optional: The Lamp Beside the Golden Door *(Offline)*

Activity 5. Optional: Welcome to America *(Offline)*

ASSESS

Lesson Assessment: The Statue of Liberty (*Online*)

You will complete an offline assessment covering the main objectives of this lesson. Your learning coach will score this assessment.

LEARN

Activity 6. Optional: Reading About the Statue of Liberty *(Offline)*

Welcome to America

Name Date

Lesson Assessment

The Statue of Liberty

1. What is a person called who leaves one country to live in another?

2. When immigrants came to the United States, what welcomed them?

3. Who gave the Statue of Liberty as a gift, and who received it?

Student Guide
Lesson 4. Optional: Immigrants to America

For many years, immigrants from all around the world have come to the United States of America seeking freedom and a better life for themselves and their children.

Lesson Objectives

- Tell that immigrants came to America from many different countries.
- Explain that immigrants faced many challenges when beginning a new life in America.
- Identify the location of the Atlantic Ocean and the Pacific Ocean.
- Tell that the Statue of Liberty welcomed immigrants to America.

PREPARE

Approximate lesson time is 45 minutes.

Materials

For the Student

map, world

crayons, 16 or more

pencils, no. 2

paper, drawing

pencils, colored, 16 or more

Optional

The Long Way to a New Land by Joan Sandin (ISBN 0064441008)

LEARN

Activity 1. Optional: Optional Lesson Instructions *(Online)*

This lesson is OPTIONAL. It is provided for students who seek enrichment or extra practice. You may skip this lesson.

If you choose to skip this lesson, then go to the Plan or Lesson Lists page and mark this lesson "Skipped" in order to proceed to the next lesson in the course.

Activity 2. Optional: A Quick Review *(Online)*

Activity 3. Optional: Jin-Song's Letters *(Online)*

Activity 4. Optional: Drawing on the Immigrant Experience *(Online)*

Activity 5. Optional: Another Immigrant's Story *(Online)*

Student Guide
Lesson 1: Thomas Alva Edison

Focus on selected Americans who changed the world with their ideas and inventions. Some, like Thomas Alva Edison, gave us the light bulb and phonograph. Others, like George Washington Carver, discovered amazing new uses for ordinary items like peanuts. Jane Addams created a place for poor people to go, and the Wright Brothers helped the nation begin to soar.

Lesson Objectives

- Identify Thomas Edison as a great inventor.
- Identify any one of the following as one of Edison's major inventions: the phonograph, movie camera, or lightbulb.

PREPARE

Approximate lesson time is 45 minutes.

Materials

For the Student

Edison's Bright Ideas

crayons, 16 or more

pencils, no. 2

Keywords and Pronunciation

incandescent (in-kuhn-DEH-suhnt)

LEARN

Activity 1: Meet Thomas Edison *(Online)*

Activity 2: Greetings from Thomas Edison *(Online)*

Activity 3. Optional: Edison's Bright Ideas *(Offline)*

ASSESS

Lesson Assessment: Thomas Alva Edison (*Online*)

You will complete an offline assessment covering the main objectives of this lesson. Your learning coach will score this assessment.

Name Date

Edison's Bright Ideas

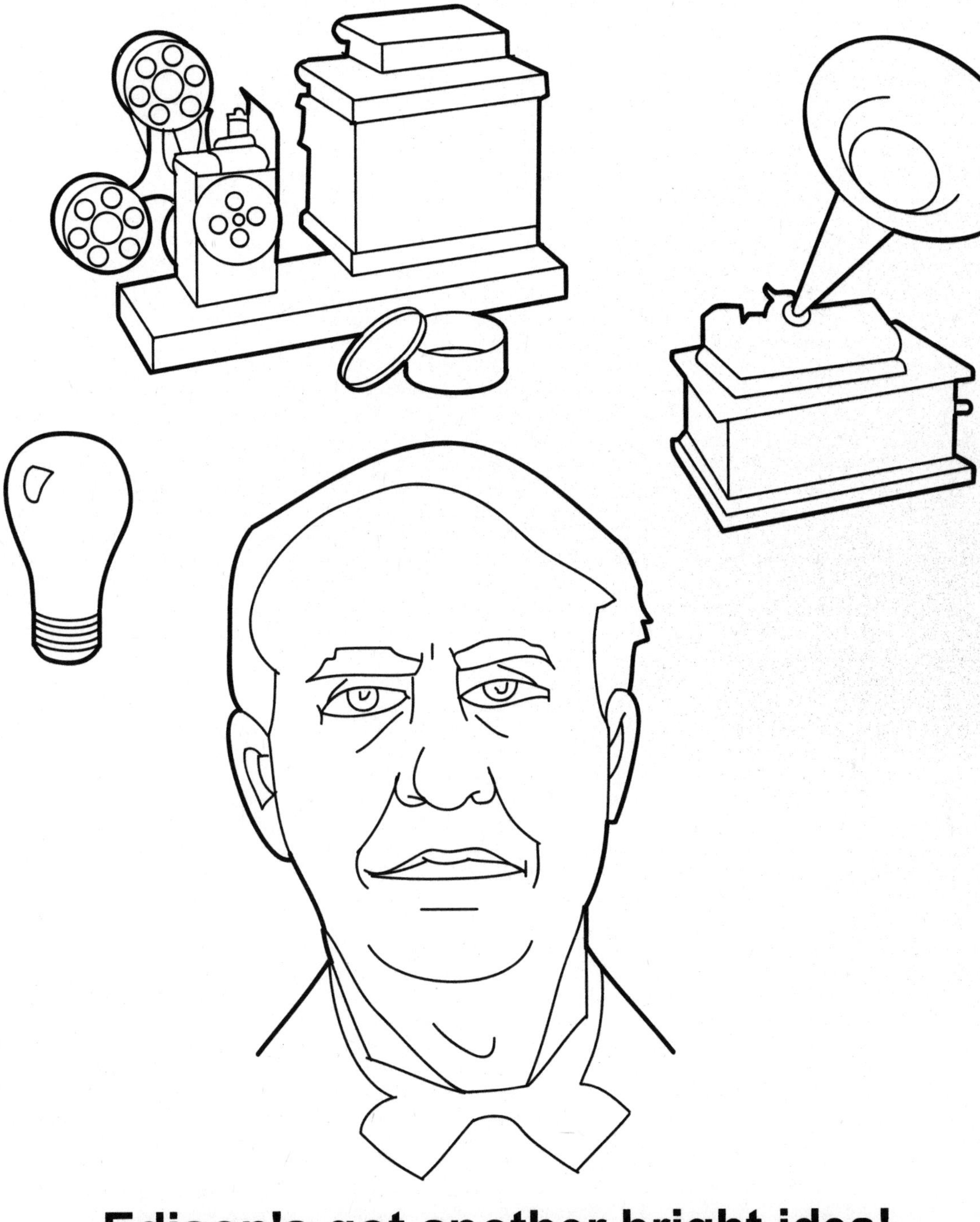

Edison's got another bright idea!

Name Date

Edison's Bright Ideas

Complete the poem about Thomas Edison using the words in the word bank. Say the poem out loud.

Edison, the inventor, had some bright ideas.
He worked long and hard, without any fears.
Think of him when you see a __________.
Thanks to his work, it will be very groovy.
He's known as the "Wizard of Menlo Park,"
Inventing the __________ with lots of spark.
Then there's the __________ and its songs,
Playing tunes, thanks to Edison, all day long.

Word Bank

movie	lightbulb	phonograph	computer	fish tank

Name Date

Lesson Assessment

Thomas Alva Edison

1. What was Thomas Edison's job?

2. Identify one of Edison's inventions.

Student Guide
Lesson 2: Theodore Roosevelt

An enthusiastic naturalist and outdoorsman, President Theodore Roosevelt preserved millions of acres of land in National Forests, Parks, and Preserves.

Lesson Objectives

- Identify George Washington as the first president of the United States of America.
- Identify Thomas Jefferson as the third president of the United States.
- Explain that Abraham Lincoln became a president of the United States.
- State that Theodore Roosevelt was a president of the United States.
- Identify the teddy bear as being named after President Roosevelt.

PREPARE

Approximate lesson time is 45 minutes.

Materials

For the Student

- Teddy Bear pattern

Optional

- Mount Rushmore activity sheet
- nickel
- quarter
- penny
- Teddy Bear Pattern
- glue sticks
- paper, colored construction, 12"x12"
- scissors, round-end safety
- crayons, 16 or more
- pencils, no. 2

LEARN

Activity 1: A Presidential Review *(Online)*

Activity 2: Theodore Roosevelt and America Grow Up *(Online)*

Activity 3: How the Teddy Bear Got Its Name *(Online)*

Activity 4: Teddy Bears *(Offline)*

ASSESS

Lesson Assessment: Theodore Roosevelt (*Online*)

You will complete an offline assessment covering the main objectives of this lesson. Your learning coach will score this assessment.

LEARN

Activity 5. Optional: Mount Rushmore *(Offline)*

cut

Name Date

Lesson Assessment

Theodore Roosevelt

1. Who was Theodore Roosevelt?
2. What was named after President Roosevelt?

Student Guide
Lesson 3: George Washington Carver

George Washington Carver discovered ways to improve plants, invented many new uses for crops, especially peanuts, and helped make small-acreage farming a profitable venture for farmers, especially in the American South.

Lesson Objectives

- Explain that George Washington Carver discovered that many things could be made from peanuts.
- Identify George Washington Carver as a teacher and scientist who helped farmers.

PREPARE

Approximate lesson time is 45 minutes.

Materials

For the Student
- Peanut Page activity sheet
- pencils, no. 2

Optional
- food - Peanuts
- Oats, Peas, Beans, and Barley Grow lyrics sheet
- George Washington Carver coloring page
- crayons, 16 or more
- A Weed is a Flower: The Life of George Washington Carver by Aliki

---

LEARN

Activity 1: The Peanut *(Online)*

Activity 2: The Life of George Washington Carver *(Online)*

Activity 3: Oats, Peas, Beans, and Barley Grow *(Offline)*

Activity 4: George Washington Carver Coloring Page *(Offline)*

ASSESS

Lesson Assessment: George Washington Carver (*Online*)

You will complete an offline assessment covering the main objectives of this lesson. Your learning coach will score this assessment.

LEARN

Activity 5. Optional: Read More *(Offline)*

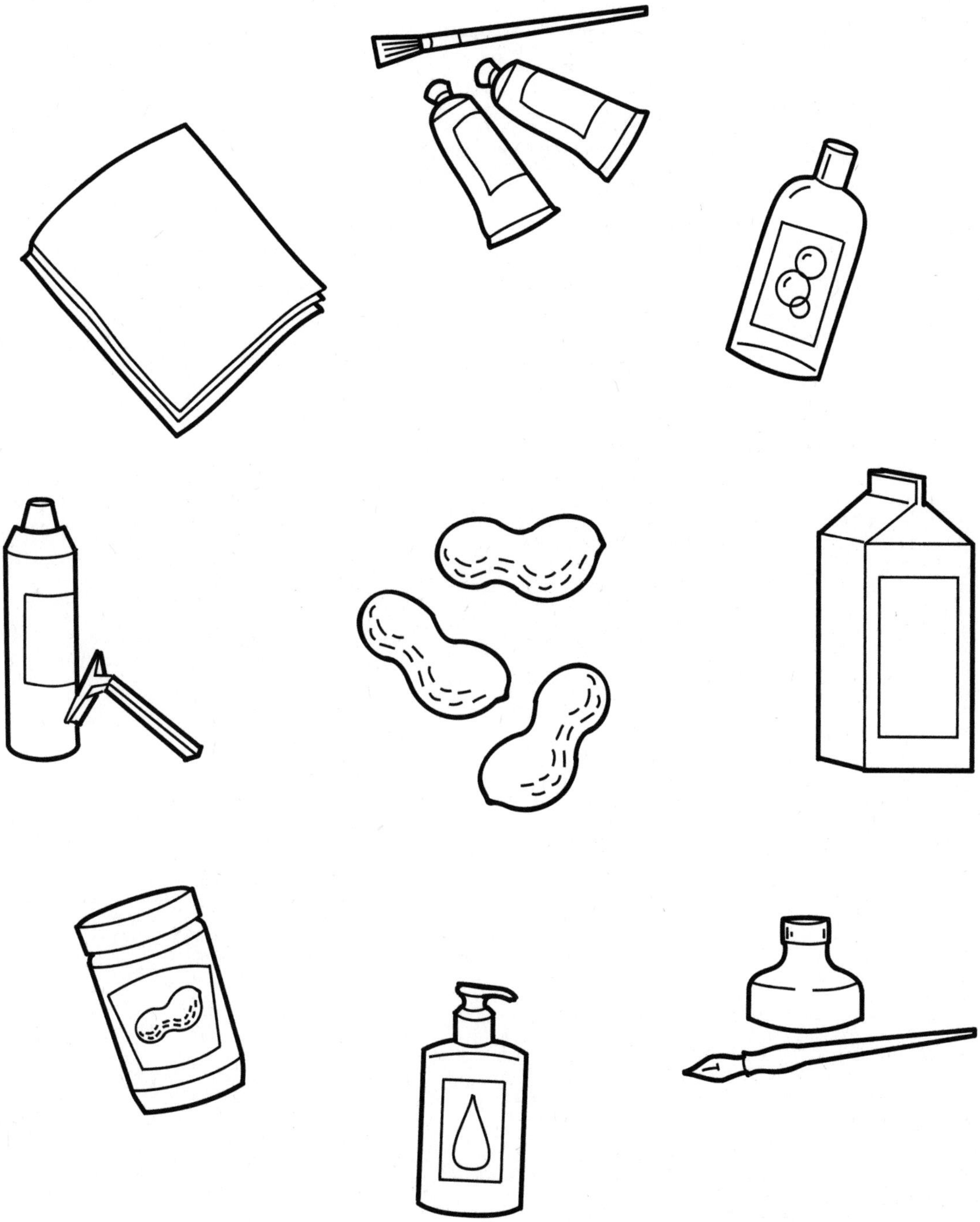

Oats, Peas, Beans, and Barley Grow

Chorus: *Skip around in a circle, or mime digging or hoeing.*
Oats, peas, beans, and barley grow,
Oats, peas, beans, and barley grow,
Can you or I or anyone know
How oats, peas, beans, and barley grow?

Verse 1: *Mime planting seeds; then standing relaxed; stamp the foot; clap hands; and finally, turn around while shading eyes.*
First the farmer sows his seeds,
Stands erect and takes his ease,
He stamps his foot and claps his hands,
And turns around to view his lands.

(Chorus)

Verse 2: *Mime watering seeds; then standing relaxed; stamp the foot; clap hands; and finally, turn around while shading eyes.*
Next the farmer waters the seeds,
Stands erect and takes his ease,
He stamps his foot and claps his hands,
And turns around to view his lands.

(Chorus)

Verse 3: *Mime hoeing weeds; then standing relaxed; stamp the foot; clap hands; and finally, turn around while shading eyes.*
Next the farmer hoes the weeds,
Stands erect and takes his ease,
He stamps his foot and claps his hands,
And turns around to view his lands.

(Chorus)

Verse 4: *Mime gathering, cutting, or carrying crops; then standing relaxed; stamp the foot; clap hands; and finally, turn around while shading eyes.*
Last the farmer harvests his seeds,
Stands erect and takes his ease,
He stamps his foot and claps his hands,
And turns around to view his lands.

(Chorus)

Name Date

Lesson Assessment

George Washington Carver

1. Who was George Washington Carver?
2. George Washington Carver discovered that many things could be made from a certain plant. What is this plant?

Student Guide
Lesson 4: Jane Addams and Hull-House

Jane Addams worked all her life to help America's urban poor, especially poor children. In 1889 she established a neighborhood center in Chicago called Hull House.

Lesson Objectives

- Identify any one of the following as one of Edison's major inventions: the phonograph, movie camera, or lightbulb.
- State that Theodore Roosevelt was a president of the United States.
- Explain that George Washington Carver discovered that many things could be made from peanuts.
- Explain that Jane Addams opened a neighborhood center called Hull-House to help poor children and families.

PREPARE

Approximate lesson time is 45 minutes.

Materials

For the Student

Optional

- Hull-House activity sheet
- The Spirit of Hull-House cut-out sheet
- crayons, 16 or more
- Elmer's Glue-All
- scissors, round-end safety
- Jane Addames: Member of the Hall of Fame Activity
- magazines - small pictures to cut
- pencils, no. 2

LEARN

Activity 1: Great Americans *(Online)*

Activity 2: Jane Addams *(Online)*

Activity 3: Remembering Hull-House *(Online)*

Activity 4. Optional: Creating Hull-House *(Offline)*

Activity 5. Optional: A Hall of Fame Experience *(Offline)*

ASSESS

Lesson Assessment: Jane Addams and Hull-House (*Online*)

You will complete an offline assessment covering the main objectives of this lesson. Your learning coach will score this assessment.

LEARN

Activity 6. Optional: What Can You Do? *(Offline)*

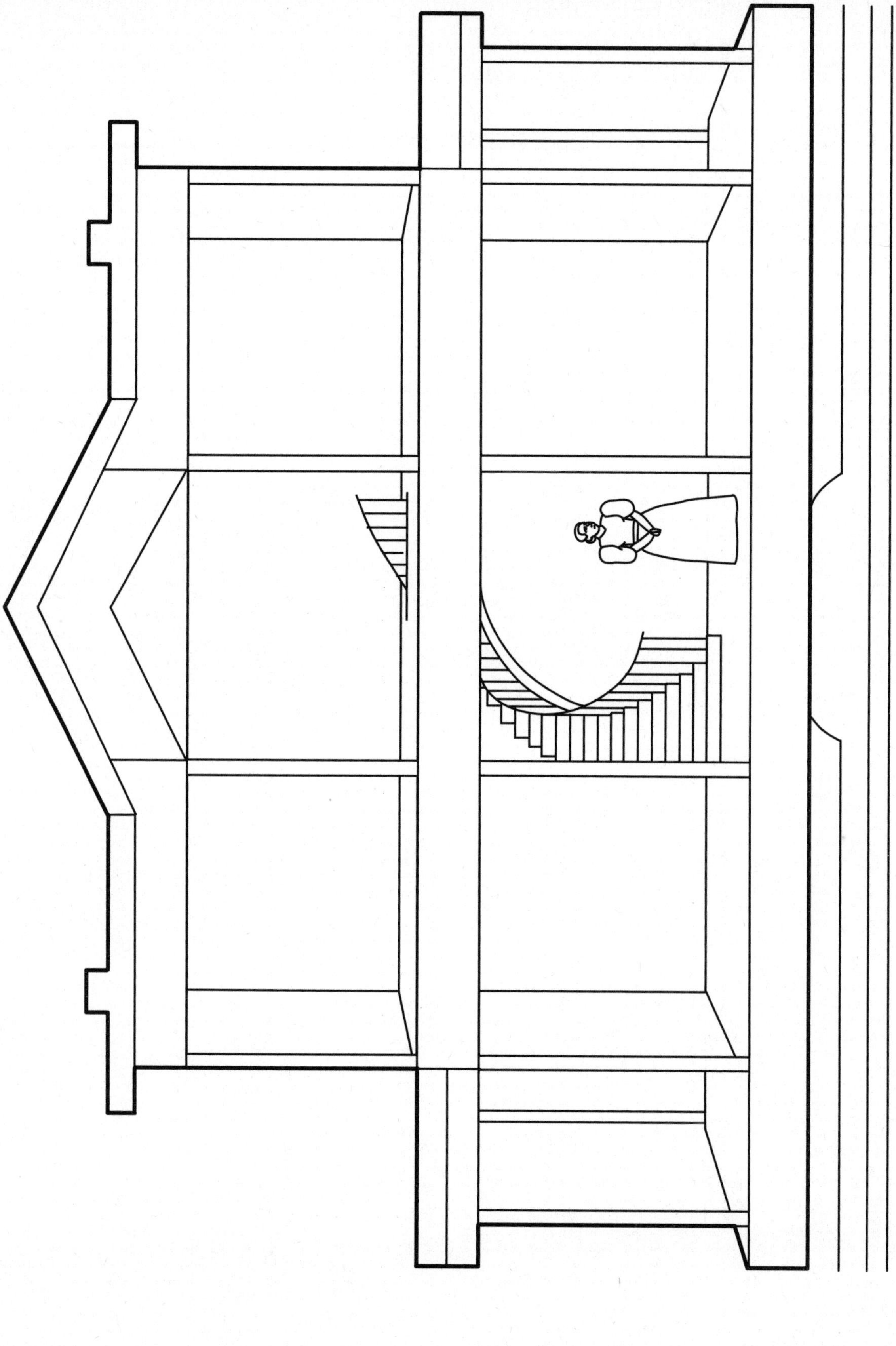

cut

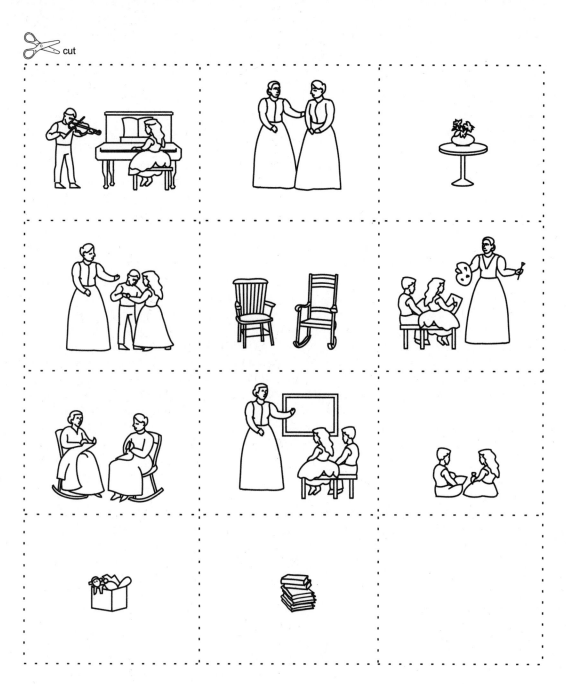

Name Date

Jane Addams: Member of the Hall of Fame

Color and decorate the space around this portrait of Jane Addams to show what she did to help people.

Name Date

Lesson Assessment

Jane Addams and Hull-House

1. Whom did Jane Addams want to help?
2. Jane Addams found a run-down old mansion in the center of a poor neighborhood to repair and use as a neighborhood center. What was its name?

Student Guide
Lesson 5. Optional: Andrew Carnegie

Lesson Objectives

- Explain that through hard work, Andrew Carnegie became a very wealthy businessman.
- Explain that Andrew Carnegie was an immigrant who came to America from Scotland.
- Describe Andrew Carnegie as a man who gave away his fortune to build libraries and do other good works.
- Identify any one of the following as one of Edison's major inventions: the phonograph, movie camera, or lightbulb.
- State that Theodore Roosevelt was a president of the United States.
- Identify George Washington Carver as a teacher and scientist who helped farmers.
- Explain that Jane Addams opened a neighborhood center called Hull-House to help poor children and families.

PREPARE

Approximate lesson time is 45 minutes.

Materials

For the Student

Andrew Carnegie Helps Others activity sheet

map, world

crayons, 16 or more

pencils, no. 2

Keywords and Pronunciation

Andrew Carnegie (KAHR-nuh-gee)

immigrant (IH muh gruhnt) : A person who comes or moves to a country to live there and make it home.

LEARN

Activity 1. Optional: Optional Lesson Instructions *(Online)*

This lesson is OPTIONAL. It is provided for students who seek enrichment or extra practice. You may skip this lesson.

If you choose to skip this lesson, then go to the Plan or Lesson Lists page and mark this lesson "Skipped" in order to proceed to the next lesson in the course.

Activity 2. Optional: Let's Review *(Online)*

Activity 3. Optional: Andrew Carnegie and the Land of Opportunity *(Online)*

Activity 4. Optional: Andrew Carnegie Travels to America *(Online)*

Activity 5. Optional: Andrew Carnegie Helps Others *(Offline)*

Activity 6. Optional: Places Andrew Carnegie Lived *(Online)*

Name ______________________ Date ______________________

Andrew Carnegie Helps Others

Andrew Carnegie thought a lot about helping others. He built museums, libraries, and other places for people to learn and enjoy. What is something you might build or do, if you were able to help others like Andrew Carnegie? Draw it in the empty bubble. Then color the rest of the pictures.

Student Guide
Lesson 6: The Wright Brothers: First to Fly

Lesson Objectives

- Identify any one of the following as one of Edison's major inventions: the phonograph, movie camera, or lightbulb.
- State that Theodore Roosevelt was a president of the United States.
- Identify George Washington Carver as a teacher and scientist who helped farmers.
- Explain that Jane Addams opened a neighborhood center called Hull-House to help poor children and families.
- Identify Orville and Wilbur Wright as the brothers who invented the first successful airplane.
- State that the Wright brothers worked together and tried many different designs before succeeding.

PREPARE

Approximate lesson time is 45 minutes.

Materials

For the Student

Fun with Flight activity sheet

Optional

The First Flight activity sheet

paper clips

paper, 8 1/2" x 11"

tape, clear

crayons, 16 or more

LEARN

Activity 1: What If? *(Online)*

Activity 2: The Dream Begins *(Online)*

Activity 3: Fun with Flight *(Offline)*

Activity 4: The Wright Brothers' First Flight *(Online)*

Activity 5. Optional: The First Flight *(Offline)*

ASSESS

Lesson Assessment: The Wright Brothers: First to Fly (*Online*)

You will complete an offline assessment covering the main objectives of this lesson. Your learning coach will score this assessment.

LEARN

Activity 6. Optional: More on the Wright Brothers *(Online)*

Fun with Flight

Follow the steps below to make and fly a paper airplane.

1. Take a sheet of paper, and fold it in half lengthwise.
2. Open the paper and fold each of the two corners at one end in until they meet at the fold line.
3. Now fold the paper in half again, with the folded down corners on the inside.
4. Take each outer edge and fold it down so that this edge is against the original center fold.
5. Tape the nose of your plane, if you like.
6. Flip up the wings. Then put a paper clip on your fold and fly your plane.

1.

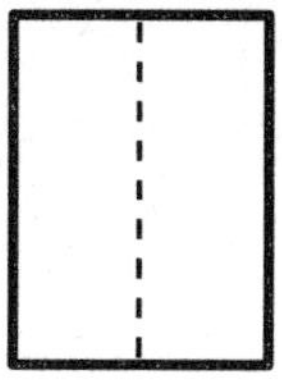

2.

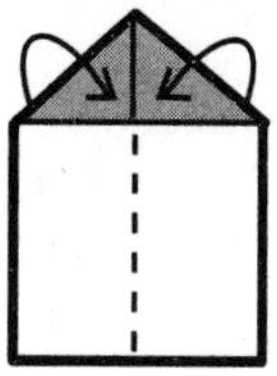

3.

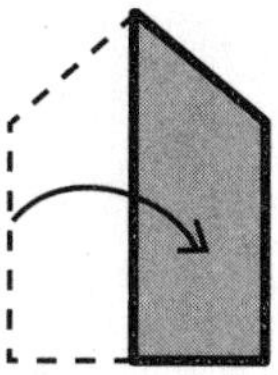

4.

5.

6.

Name ______________________________ Date ______________________________

The First Flight, Kitty Hawk, North Carolina

Color the picture of Orville and Wilbur Wright at their first flight at Kitty Hawk, North Carolina. Would you have wanted to be Orville or Wilbur on that day? Circle the name of the Wright brother who was doing what you would have wanted to do.

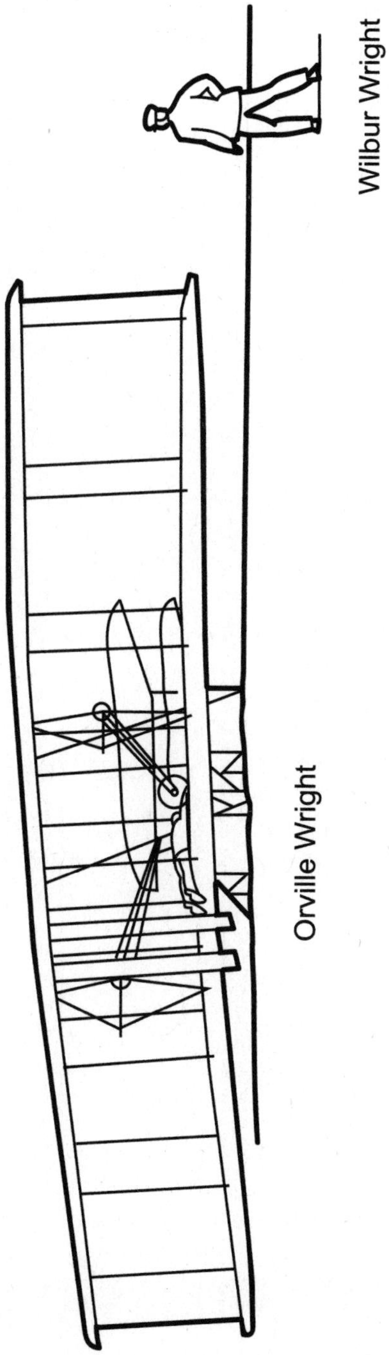

Name Date

Lesson Assessment

The Wright Brothers: First to Fly

1. Who were the brothers who invented the first successful airplane?

2. How many attempts did the Wright Brothers have before creating the first successful plane?

Student Guide
Lesson 7: Dorothy Harrison Eustis

Lesson Objectives

- Identify Sequoyah as the Cherokee Indian who invented a way of writing the Cherokee language.
- Identify Thomas Hopkins Gallaudet as the person who started the first American school for deaf children.
- Identify Harriet Tubman as a woman who escaped from slavery and helped others do the same.
- Identify Susan B. Anthony as a woman who worked for women's rights.
- Name Dorothy Harrison Eustis as the person who started a school for guide dogs for the blind.
- Identify the guide dogs described in the lesson as Seeing Eye dogs.

PREPARE

Approximate lesson time is 45 minutes.

Materials

For the Student

Buddy Helps coloring sheet

crayons, 16 or more

LEARN

Activity 1: Think About Helping Others *(Online)*

Activity 2: The Seeing Eye *(Online)*

Activity 3: A Buddy for the Blind *(Offline)*

ASSESS

Lesson Assessment: Dorothy Harrison Eustis (*Online*)

You will complete an offline assessment covering the main objectives of this lesson. Your learning coach will score this assessment.

LEARN
Activity 4: Review *(Online)*

Name ______________________ Date ______________________

Buddy Helps

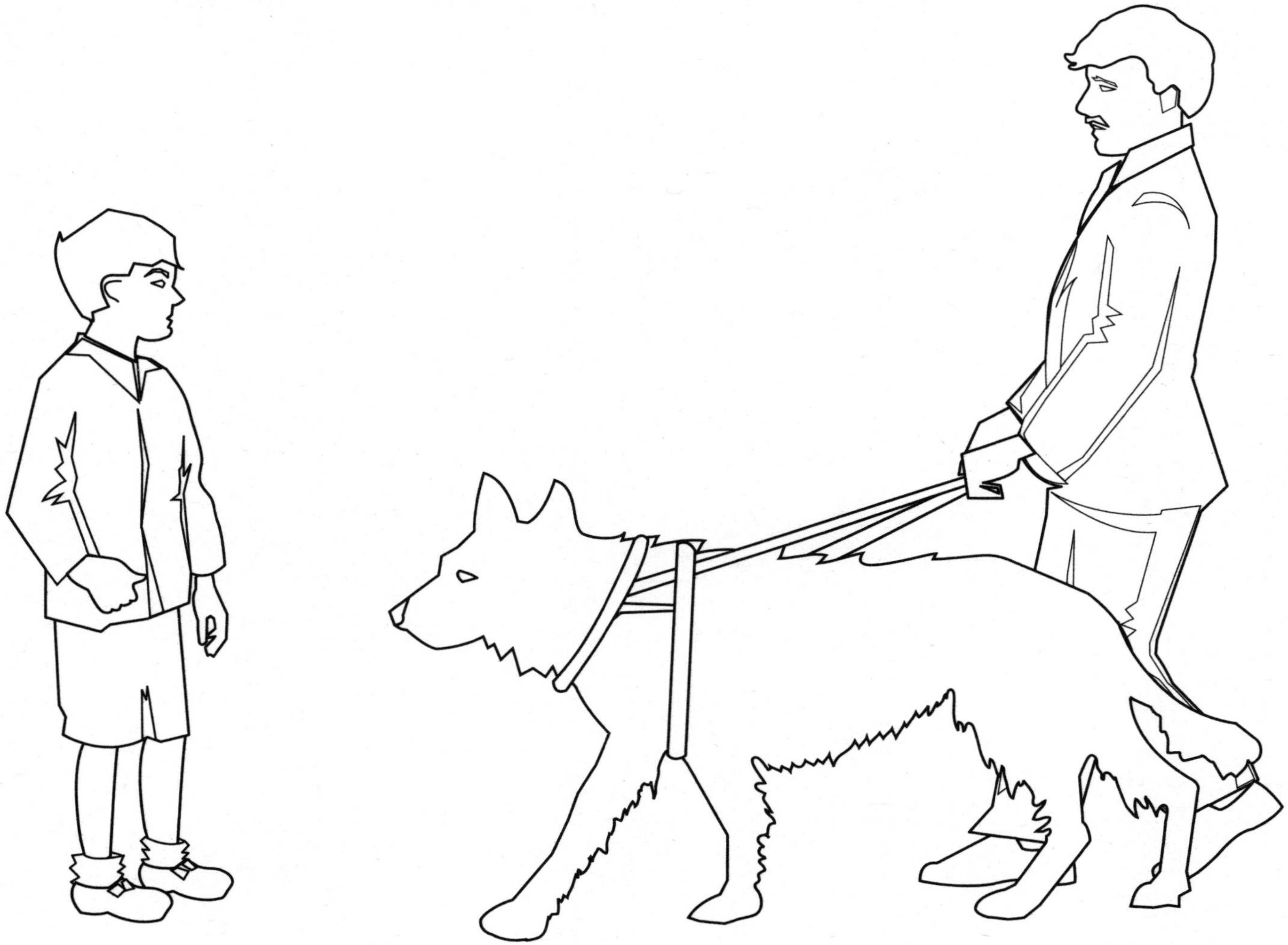

Name Date

Lesson Assessment

Dorothy Harrison Eustis

1. What was the name of the person who trained dogs to help guide the blind?
2. What were the dogs who helped guide the blind called?

Student Guide

Lesson 1: Eleanor Roosevelt: "First Lady of the World"

In modern times, dedicated leaders like Eleanor Roosevelt, Dr. Martin Luther King Jr., and Cesar Chavez worked to ensure freedom for many different people. Others, such as baseball player Jackie Robinson and seamstress Rosa Parks, also took courageous stands to further those goals.

Lesson Objectives

- Describe Eleanor Roosevelt as a woman who worked all her life to help others.
- Describe Lincoln as a man known for his honesty.
- Explain that Abraham Lincoln grew up as a pioneer.
- Explain that Lincoln believed slavery was wrong.
- Explain that the president's wife is called "The First Lady."
- Identify George Washington as a person known for his honesty
- Identify George Washington as the first president of the United States of America.
- Identify the teddy bear as being named after President Roosevelt.
- Recall that Thomas Jefferson wrote the Declaration of Independence.
- State that Theodore Roosevelt was a president of the United States.

PREPARE

Approximate lesson time is 45 minutes.

Materials

For the Student

- First Lady Footprints pattern sheet
- Mount Rushmore activity sheet
- globe, inflatable
- crayons, 16 or more
- Elmer's Glue-All
- glitter

Optional

- A Picture Book of Eleanor Roosevelt by David A. Adler
- Amelia and Eleanor Go for a Ride by Pam Munoz Ryan

LEARN

Activity 1: Past Presidents *(Online)*

Activity 2: Young Eleanor in Italy *(Online)*

Activity 3: Eleanor Roosevelt: Beloved First Lady *(Online)*

Activity 4: First Lady of the World *(Offline)*

ASSESS

Lesson Assessment: Eleanor Roosevelt: "First Lady of the World" (*Online*)

You will complete an offline assessment covering the main objectives of this lesson. Your learning coach will score this assessment.

LEARN

Activity 5. Optional: Read More About Eleanor Roosevelt *(Offline)*

Name Date

First Lady Footprints

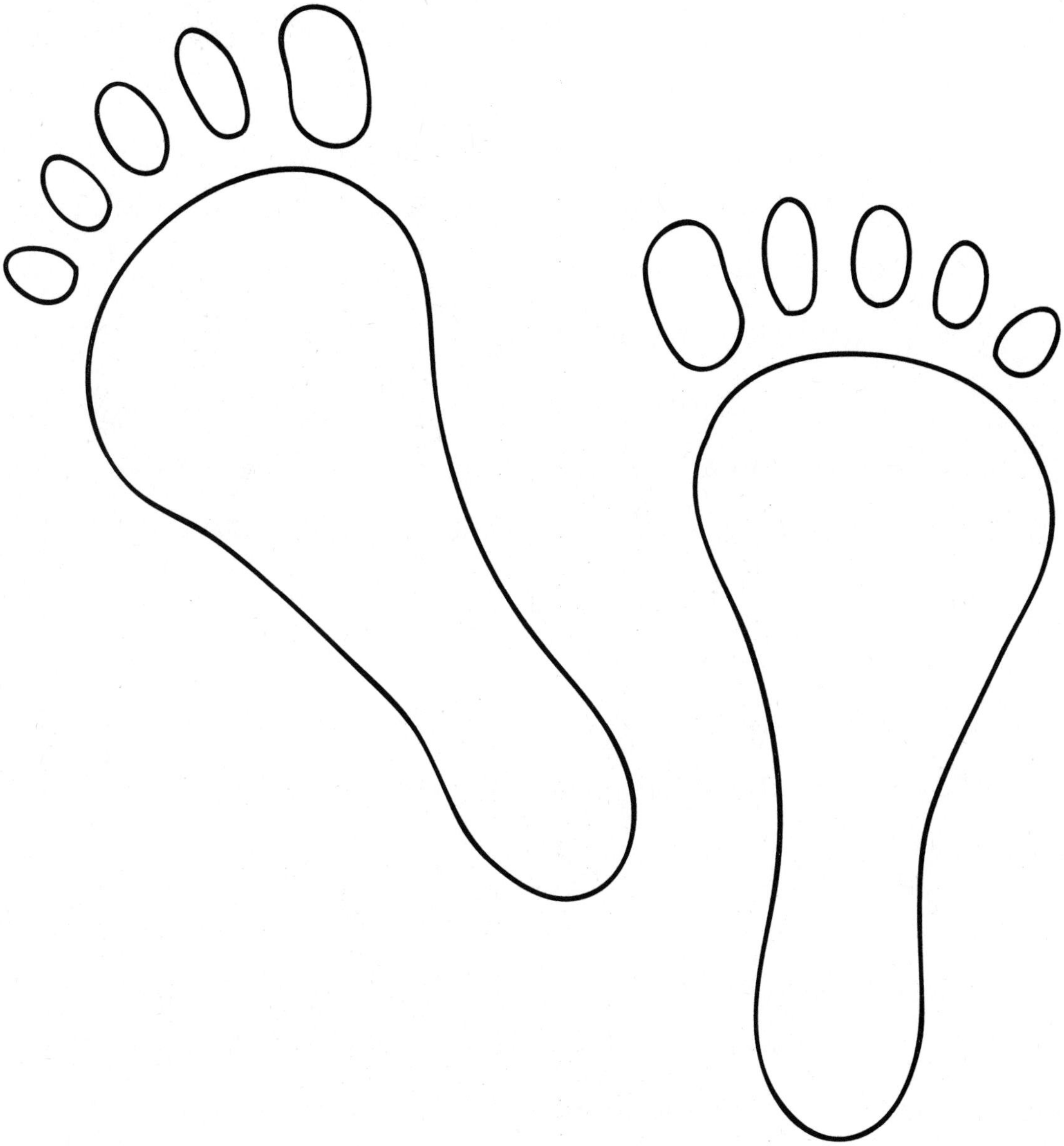

Name Date

Lesson Assessment

Eleanor Roosevelt: "First Lady of the World"

1. What is the president's wife called?

2. What did Eleanor Roosevelt do most of her life?

Student Guide
Lesson 2: Jackie Robinson

Lesson Objectives

- Name Jackie Robinson as the first black baseball player to play in the Major Leagues.

PREPARE

Approximate lesson time is 45 minutes.

Materials

For the Student

- *Take Me Out to the Ball Game* lyrics sheet
- Dodgers Pennant coloring page
- Take Me Out to the Ball Game lyrics sheet
- dowel
- crayons, 16 or more
- Elmer's Glue-All
- scissors, round-end safety
- tape, clear

Optional

- A Picture Book of Jackie Robinson by David A. Adler

LEARN

Activity 1: America's Pastime *(Online)*

Activity 2: Jackie Robinson Changes Baseball *(Online)*

Activity 3: Jackie Robinson &the Dodgers' Pennant *(Offline)*

Activity 4. Optional: This Time with Gusto *(Offline)*

ASSESS

Lesson Assessment: Jackie Robinson (*Online*)

You will complete an offline assessment covering the main objectives of this lesson. Your learning coach will score this assessment.

LEARN

Activity 5. Optional: Jackie Robinson Picture Book *(Offline)*

Take Me Out to the Ball Game

Take me out to the ball game,
Take me out to the crowd.
Buy me some peanuts and Cracker Jacks,
I don't care if I never get back,
We'll just root, root, root for the home team,
If they don't win, it's a shame,
'Cause it's ONE, TWO, THREE strikes you're out
At the old ball game!

BROOKLYN
Dodgers
WORLD
CHAMPIONS

Name ______________________________ Date ______________________________

Lesson Assessment

Jackie Robinson

1. Who was the first black baseball player to play for the Major Leagues?

Student Guide
Lesson 3: Cesar Chavez: "Yes, it can be done!"

Lesson Objectives

- Explain that Cesar Chavez won better conditions for migrant farm workers.

PREPARE

Approximate lesson time is 45 minutes.

Materials

For the Student

map of U.S. Crop Regions

Optional

Better Conditions coloring page

map, U.S.

crayons, 16 or more

Cesar Chavez: a Photo-Illustrated Biography by Lucile Davis

Keywords and Pronunciation

César Chávez (SAY-sahr CHAHV-ez)

Si, se puede (see, say PWAY-day)

LEARN

Activity 1: Where Are They Grown? *(Online)*

Activity 2: Harvest Time *(Online)*

Activity 3: Cesar Chavez: "Yes, it can be done!" *(Online)*

Activity 4: Places from Cesar's Life *(Online)*

Activity 5. Optional: Better Conditions for Migrant Farm Workers *(Offline)*

ASSESS

Lesson Assessment: Cesar Chavez: "Yes, it can be done!" (*Online*)

You will complete an offline assessment covering the main objectives of this lesson. Your learning coach will score this assessment

LEARN
Activity 6. Optional: Cesar Chavez in Photographs *(Offline)*

U.S. Crop Regions

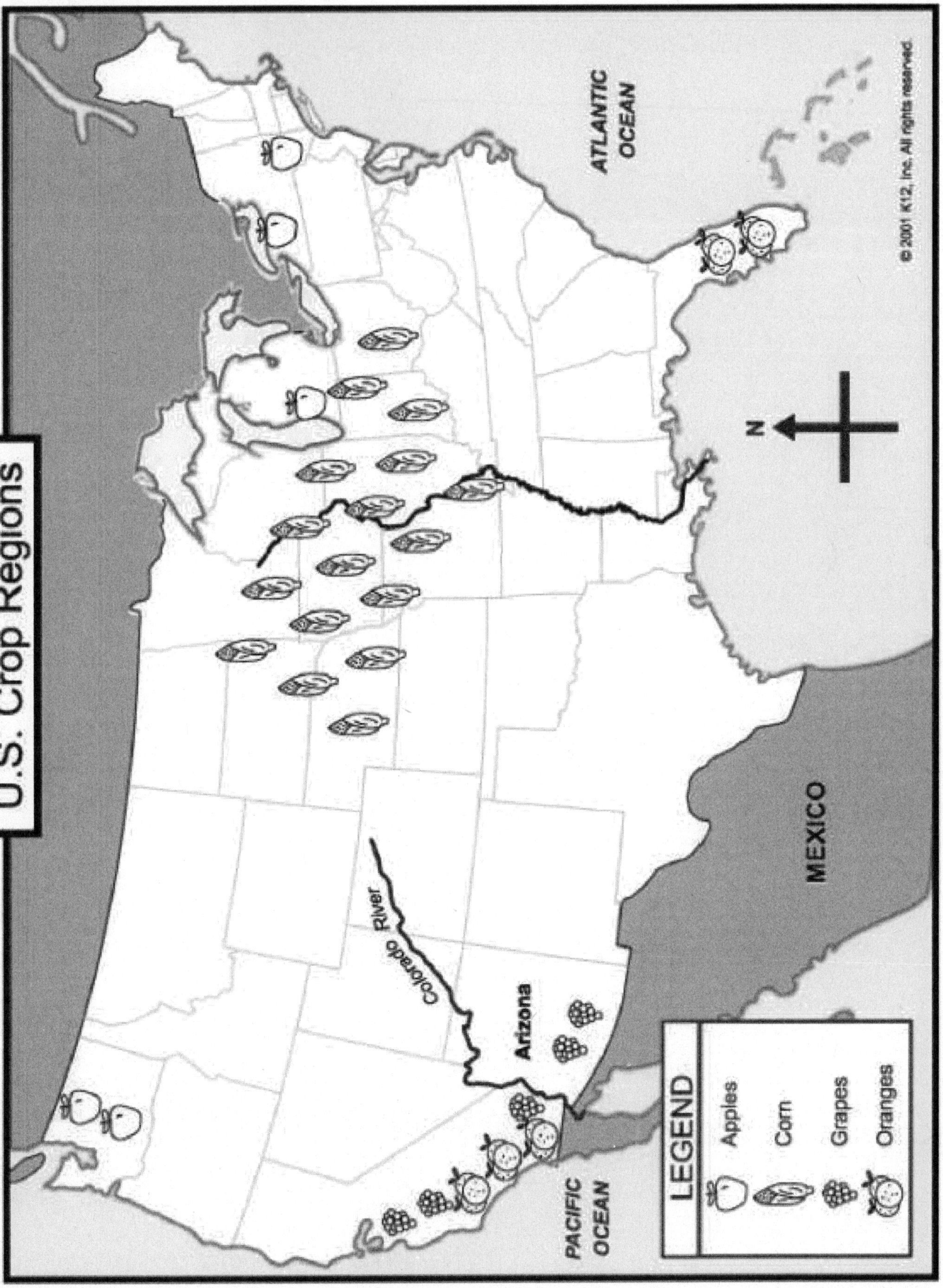

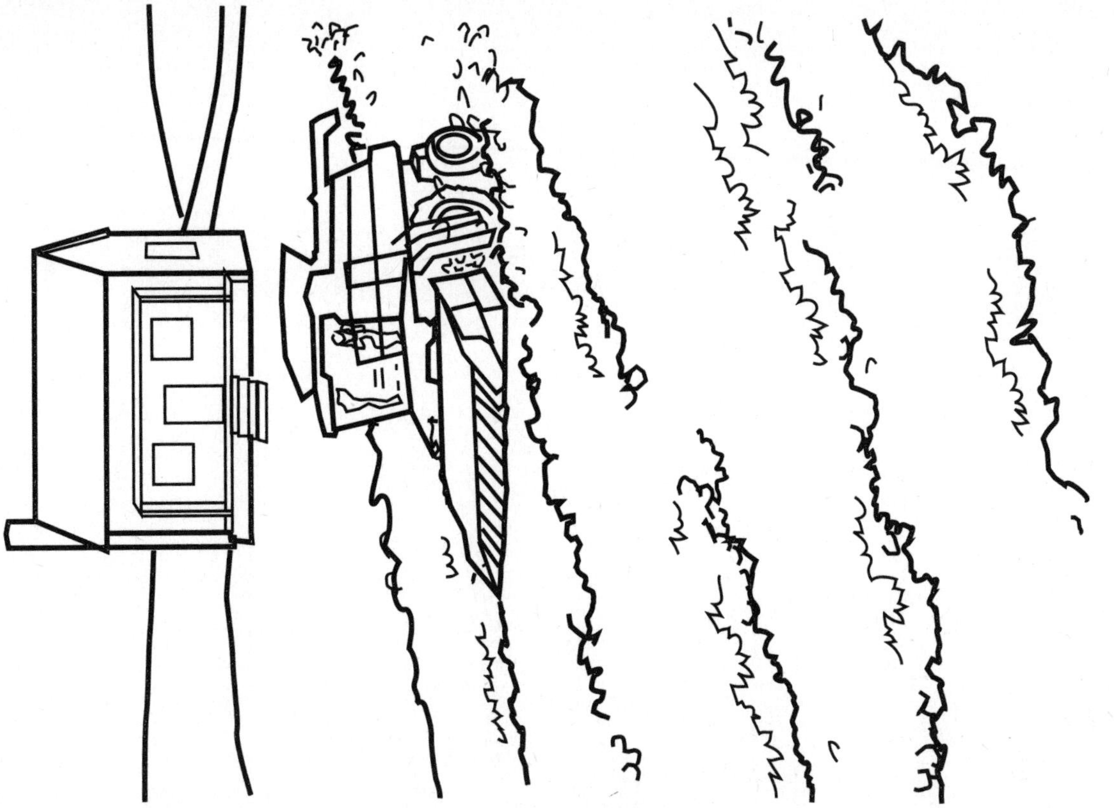

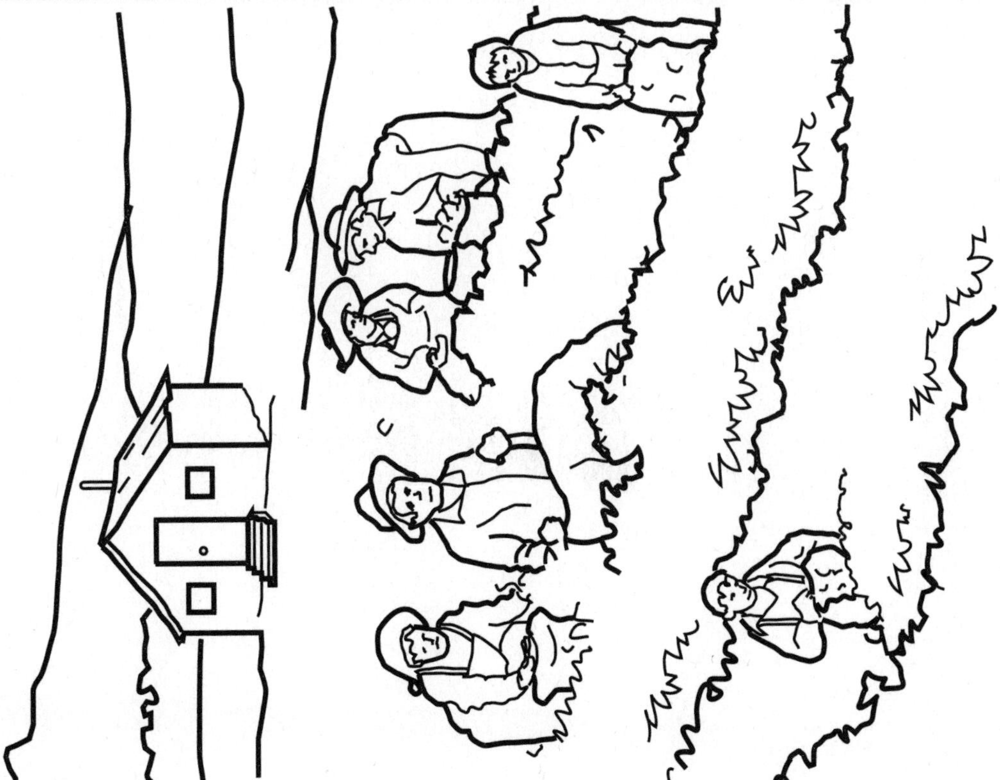

Name Date

Lesson Assessment

Cesar Chavez: "Yes, it can be done!"

1. Who won better conditions for migrant farm workers?

Student Guide
Lesson 4: Rosa Parks and Dr. Martin Luther King Jr.

Lesson Objectives

- Describe Rosa Parks as a brave woman who would not give up her seat to a white man on a bus.
- Identify Dr. Martin Luther King Jr. as a leader of a peaceful movement to ensure that all people are treated fairly.

PREPARE

Approximate lesson time is 45 minutes.

Materials

For the Student

- My Country 'Tis of Thee lyrics sheet

Optional

- We All Sit Together activity sheet
- magazines
- pencils, no. 2
- crayons, 16 or more
- Elmer's Glue-All
- scissors, round-end safety
- tape, clear
- A Picture Book of Rosa Parks by David A. Adler
- Dr. Martin Luther King, Jr. by David A. Adler
- Happy Birthday, Martin Luther King by Jean Marzollo
- I Am Rosa Parks by Rosa Parks and James Haskins

LEARN

Activity 1: Let Freedom Ring *(Online)*

Activity 2: A History of Freedom *(Online)*

Activity 3: Rosa Parks Says "No" *(Online)*

Activity 4. Optional: We All Sit Together *(Offline)*

Activity 5: The Dream of Martin Luther King Jr. *(Online)*

Activity 6: American Leaders *(Online)*

ASSESS

Lesson Assessment: Rosa Parks and Dr. Martin Luther King Jr. (*Online*)

You will complete an offline assessment covering the main objectives of this lesson. Your learning coach will score this assessment.

LEARN

Activity 7. Optional: Reading More About Parks and King *(Offline)*

My Country, 'Tis of Thee

My country, 'tis of thee,
Sweet land of liberty,
Of thee I sing.
Land where my fathers died,
Land of the pilgrim's pride,
From every mountainside,
Let freedom ring.

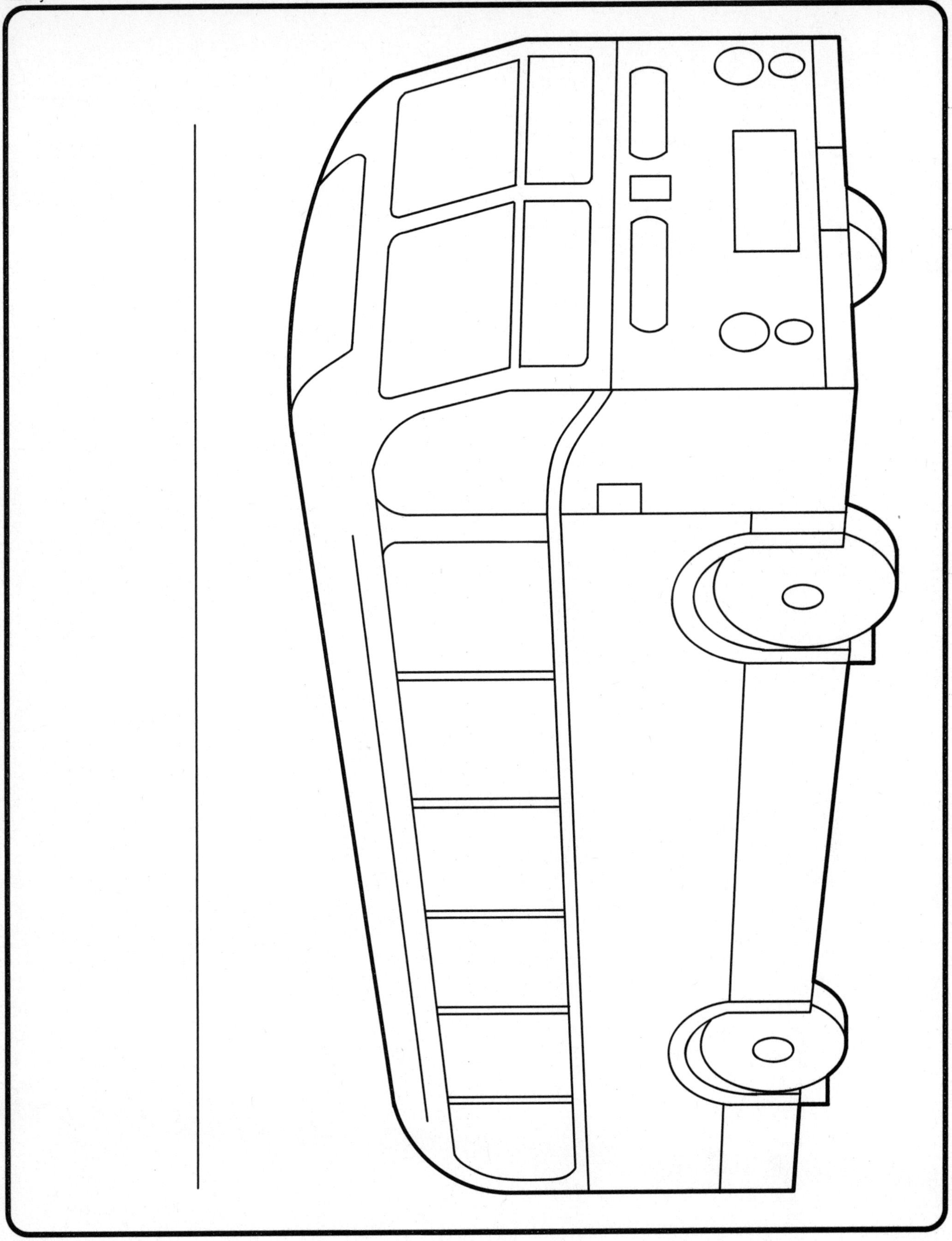

Name Date

Lesson Assessment

Rosa Parks and Dr. Martin Luther King Jr.

1. Who was Rosa Parks?

2. Who was Dr. Martin Luther King Jr.?

Answer Keys

Name Date

Lesson Assessment Answer Key

Christopher Columbus

Answers

1. Christopher Columbus
2. He thought he had landed in the islands called "the Indies".
3. *Niña*, *Pinta* and *Santa María*

Name Date

Lesson Assessment Answer Key

The Pilgrims' First Thanksgiving

Answers:

1. the Pilgrims
2. the *Mayflower*
3. Squanto
4. the Pilgrims and the Wampanoag Indians

Name Date

Lesson Assessment Answer Key

Thirteen English Colonies and the Story of William Penn

Answers:

1. William Penn
2. for religious freedom
3. thirteen
4. the Atlantic Ocean

Name Date

Lesson Assessment Answer Key

Junípero Serra in California

Answers:

1. He was a Spanish priest.
2. He started missions in what is now California.

Name Date

Lesson Assessment Answer Key

"Yankee Doodle" - The American Revolution

Answers:

1. 13
2. England
3. Answers may vary but could include: they declared their independence; they broke away from England; they became their own country.
4. a democracy
5. the American Revolution

Name Date

Lesson Assessment Answer Key

Betsy Ross and the First American Flag

Answers:

1. The United States of America
2. The American flag has 13 red and white stripes.
3. The 13 red and white stripes represent the original thirteen colonies.
4. The American flag has 50 stars.
5. The 50 stars stand for the 50 states in the United States of America.
6. Betsy Ross

Name Date

Lesson Assessment Answer Key

George Washington

Answers:

1. George Washington was the first president of the United States of America.
2. George Washington was a person known for his honesty.

Name Date

Lesson Assessment Answer Key

Thomas Jefferson

Answers:

1. Thomas Jefferson wrote the Declaration of Independence.

2. Thomas Jefferson was the third president of the United States.

Name Date

Lesson Assessment Answer Key

Johnny Appleseed

Answers:

1. When the United States was new, many people moved westward.
2. Johnny Appleseed was a man who traveled westward planting apple trees along his way.

Name Date

Lesson Assessment Answer Key

Lewis and Clark and Sacagawea

Answers:

1. Lewis and Clark were the leaders of an important voyage of exploration in the American West.
2. Sacagawea was a young Shoshone woman who helped Lewis and Clark during their journey.
3. The Mississippi River is in the center of the United States.
4. The Rocky Mountains are to the west of the Mississippi River in the United States.
5. The Pacific Ocean is to the west of the United States.

Name Date

Lesson Assessment Answer Key

Paul Bunyan

Answers:

1. Paul Bunyan was a legendary lumberjack.
2. A tall tale is an exaggerated, make-believe story.
3. Pioneers kept traveling west, all the way to California

Name Date

Lesson Assessment Answer Key

Sequoyah's Great Invention

Answers:

1. Writing is important because people can us it to tell stories, send news, and leave messages.

2. Sequoyah was the Cherokee Indian who invented a way of writing the Cherokee language.

Name Date

Lesson Assessment Answer Key

Thomas Hopkins Gallaudet

Answers:

1. A deaf person cannot hear.

2. Thomas Hopkins Gallaudet was the person who started the first American school for deaf children.

3. Many deaf people use American Sign Language to communicate.

Name Date

Lesson Assessment Answer Key

Harriet Tubman and the Underground Railroad

Answers:

1. Harriet Tubman was a woman who escaped from slavery and helped others do the same.
2. Slaves traveled north by following the stars of the Drinking Gourd (or Big Dipper) to freedom.
3. The Underground Railroad was not a real railroad but a way for slaves to get to the North and become free.

Name Date

Lesson Assessment Answer Key

"Honest Abe": Abraham Lincoln

Answers:

1. pioneers
2. a president of the United States
3. honesty
4. It was wrong.
5. the Lincoln Memorial

Name Date

Lesson Assessment Answer Key

Susan B. Anthony: Women's Rights

Answers:

1. Susan B. Anthony.
2. Susan B. Anthony worked hard to get women the right to vote.

Name Date

Lesson Assessment Answer Key

Laura Ingalls Wilder

Answers:

1. A pioneer was an early settler of the American West.
2. Laura Ingalls Wilder was a pioneer who grew up to become an author.
3. Like pioneers, Laura and her family were early settlers of the American West.

Name Date

Lesson Assessment Answer Key

John Henry and the Railroad

Answers:

1. John Henry
2. railroad worker
3. John Henry was a very large and very strong man, who could work very fast.
4. John won the battle, but he worked so hard his heart gave out.

Name Date

Lesson Assessment Answer Key

The Statue of Liberty

Answers:

1. An immigrant as a person who leaves one country to live in another.
2. The Statue of Liberty
3. The Statue of Liberty was a gift from France to the United States.

Name Date

Lesson Assessment Answer Key

Thomas Alva Edison

Answers:

1. Thomas Edison was an inventor.
2. All of the following were Edison's major inventions: the phonograph, the movie camera, and the incandescent light bulb.

Name Date

Lesson Assessment Answer Key

Theodore Roosevelt

Answers:

1. a president of the United States
2. teddy bears

Name Date

Lesson Assessment Answer Key

George Washington Carver

Answers:

1. a teacher and scientist who helped farmers
2. peanut

Name Date

Lesson Assessment Answer Key

Jane Addams and Hull-House

Answers:

1. poor children and families
2. Hull-House

Name Date

Lesson Assessment Answer Key

The Wright Brothers: First to Fly

Answers:

1. Orville and Wilbur Wright; the Wright brothers
2. There is no correct number, we just know the Wright brothers worked together and tried many different designs before succeeding.

Name Date

Lesson Assessment Answer Key

Dorothy Harrison Eustis

Answers:

1. Dorothy Harrison Eustis
2. Seeing Eye dogs or guide dogs

Name Date

Lesson Assessment Answer Key

Eleanor Roosevelt: "First Lady of the World"

Answers:

1. The president's wife is called "The First Lady."
2. Eleanor Roosevelt was a woman who worked all her life to help others.

Name Date

Lesson Assessment Answer Key

Jackie Robinson

Answers:

1. Jackie Robinson was the first black baseball player to play in the Major Leagues.

Name Date

Lesson Assessment Answer Key

Cesar Chavez: "Yes, it can be done!"

Answers:

1. Cesar Chavez won better conditions for migrant farm workers.

Name Date

Lesson Assessment Answer Key

Rosa Parks and Dr. Martin Luther King Jr.

Answers:

1. Rosa Parks was a brave woman who would not give up her seat to a white man on a bus.
2. Dr. Martin Luther King Jr. was a leader of a peaceful movement to ensure that all people are treated fairly.